ECUMENICAL STUDIES IN HISTORY
No. 1

THE GERMAN CHURCH CONFLICT

by

KARL BARTH

LUTTERWORTH PRESS

LONDON

ECUMENICAL STUDIES IN HISTORY

The purpose of this series is to examine afresh problems of Church History and to do this for the sake of Church Unity. The subjects are drawn from many periods, places and communions. Their unity lies not in a common outlook of the writers, nor in a common method of treatment. It lies solely in the aim of, in one way or another, directly or indirectly, furthering the unity of the Church. The contributors are no less diverse than the subjects, and represent many Churches, nations and races.

General Editors

THE REV. A. M. ALLCHIN, Pusey House, Oxford

THE REV. MARTIN E. MARTY PH.D., University of Chicago.

THE REV. T. H. L. PARKER, D.D., Oakington Vicarage, Cambridge

Advisory Board

DR. G. V. BENNETT, New College, Oxford.

PROFESSOR OWEN CHADWICK, Selwyn College, Cambridge.

PRINCIPAL RUSSELL CHANDRAN, United Theological College, Bangalore, S. India.

PROFESSOR HORTON DAVIES, Princeton University, U.S.A.

FATHER B. D. DUPUY, O.P., Catholic Theological Faculty, Le Saulchoir, Paris.

PROFESSOR CHARLES FORMAN, Yale Divinity School, U.S.A.

FATHER BERNARD LEEMING, S. J., Heythrop College, Chipping Norton, England.

PROFESSOR J. D. MCCAUGHEY, Ormond College, Melbourne, Australia.

PROFESSOR JAMES MACEWEN, University of Aberdeen, Scotland.

PROFESSOR JAMES SMYLIE, Union Theological Seminary, Richmond, Virginia, U.S.A.

PROFESSOR RICHARD STAUFFER, Protesttan Theological Faculty, Paris.

PROFESSOR BENGT SUNDKLER, Uppsala, Sweden.

PROFESSOR HARRY SAWYERR, University College, Sierra Leone.

PROFESSOR MARTIN SCHMIDT, University of Mainz, Germany.

CONTENTS

First published in English 1965
© 1956 CHR. KAISER VERLAG, MÜNCHEN, GERMANY.
ENGLISH TRANSLATION © 1965 LUTTERWORTH PRESS

This book originally appeared in German as *Karl Barth zum Kirchen-kampf* (edited E. Wolf) and was Number 49 in *Theologische Existenz heute, Neue Folge.* (Chr. Kaiser Verlag, München, 1956). It was translated by P. T. A. Parker.

LUTTERWORTH PRESS
4 BOUVERIE STREET, LONDON, E.C.4

JOHN KNOX PRESS
RICHMOND, VIRGINIA, U.S.A.

*Printed in Great Britain by
Latimer Trend & Co Ltd, Plymouth*

EDITOR'S INTRODUCTION

KARL BARTH WAS closely implicated in the conflict between Church and State in Germany from the beginning. When the National Socialists came to power in 1933 he was professor in Bonn, and was, therefore, and had been for twelve years, as he points out (on p. 25) a member of the Church in Germany. So long as he remained there, he took a leading part in rallying and equipping the Church for resistance. But in 1935 he was deported to his native land and perforce could only continue from the outside. That he did so continue, however, this book bears witness.

How are we to describe this collection of essays? As an account of the conflict, it is very slight, although it has a certain historical value in having been written by a leading participant of the calibre of Barth. Again, as documents for what I suppose we must now call "Barth-study", the pieces are undoubtedly of great importance in illustrating the political implications of his theology. It was for neither of these two reasons that we chose it as one of the first two numbers in the series of *Ecumenical Studies in History*, but rather because it speaks both directly and indirectly to the ecumenical situation today—not least in Great Britain and the United States of America.

First (ultimately this is the less important of the two), its direct relevance. One of the major issues in the earlier part of the struggle was the attempt by the State, acting through the German-Christians, to unify the Church in Germany. There were those who welcomed this as a step in the right ecumenical direction. The four hundred year old bitter struggle between Lutherans and Calvinists might be ended at a stroke. But there were also not lacking dyed in the wool conservatives —Luther right or wrong! Calvin right or wrong!—who would have none of this. The Confessing Church was put in the awkward position of desiring Church unity but seeming to be enemies of unity.

Nevertheless, peace at any price was resisted. Barth's answer is based on honesty towards the other side and towards one's own conscience. "No compromise!" he says here, as he also said to the Church of Scotland during the Conversations with the Church of England. Those who are ready for re-union at any price should ponder the fact that it is precisely this intransigence (the famous Barthian intransigence that everyone apparently hated so much in the twenties and then suddenly admired as the doughtiness of a "bonny fighter" in the thirties) that could not only bridge the gap between Lutherans and Reformed in the German Confessing Church, but could also establish a genuine *rapprochement* with Rome.

We come to the indirect relevance of this book to our own situation. "No compromise!" is only the negative counterpart of confession to Jesus Christ. To confess to Christ means not to confess to others than Christ. And since He is the objective unity of the Church, who makes both one, confession to Him is the subjective unity of the Church. Those who confess to Him are already one. Their one-ness is so much the more genuine and real in proportion as they confess to Him and not to "another".

Now, the heart of the German Church struggle lay in the confessing of Jesus Christ. This is the contribution, the decisive contribution, that Barth was enabled to supply from his understanding of the Gospel. Long before 1933 and quite independently of political considerations, he had learned that man's way consists in following God's way—concretely, in becoming aware and confessing that "Jesus Christ, as witnessed by the Scripture, is the one Word of God which we hear and obey and in which we trust in life and death" (Declaration of Barmen). When the time came, all he had to do was to apply this central truth to the new situation. Witness to Jesus Christ alone meant, under the Third Reich, the denial of the Neo-German paganism and of the German-Christian heresy. Certainly, we are in a totally different situation, yet as we read this book, we find our own situation remarkably mirrored in it. It may be that our way forward is also to be found in it, the way of confession to Jesus Christ alone. He is the objective unity of the Church; confession to Him is the Church's subjective unity.

NOTES

These nine pieces, written between 1933 and 1939, come (apart from 1 and 6) from two sources. *Theologische Existenz heute* (quoted as Theol. Ex. h.) was the name of a series started by Barth in 1933, replacing the earlier series *Zwischen den Zeiten*. All the pieces in 3 are from Forewords to various numbers. The remaining articles appeared in *Zwingli-Kalender*, an annual production in Basel.

The fuller story of the Confessing Church may be learned from A. S. Duncan-Jones: *The Struggle for Religious Freedom in Germany*. (London, 1938). Quoted as Duncan-Jones.

W. Gurian: *Hitler and the Christians*. London, 1936.
A. Frey: *Cross and Swastika*. London, 1938.
In German there is the thorough
   Arbeiten zur Geschichte des Kirchenkampfes. Herausgeg. v. K.D.
      Schmidt. 11 vols. 1958–63. Göttingen. (Quoted as AGK).
Vol. I is a bibliography containing no less than 5,566 entries.

All the footnotes are editorial. The Editor has not thought it necessary
or desirable to supply notes to allusions which might wound reputa-
tions.

Our thanks are due to Pastor von Rabenau of the German Lutheran
Church in Cambridge for elucidating two stubborn bits of translation.

Oakington, 1964.   T. H. L. Parker.

I

CONFLICT IN THE CHURCH[1]

WHOEVER PICKS UP this essay is advised first of all to read carefully through the fifteenth chapter of the Acts of the Apostles, verses 1–35. This chapter is important and instructive in more than one respect; it also contains a few riddles and difficulties. At any rate, one of the reasons why it concerns us is that it tells of a conflict in the Church. The Church of today, our Church, has good reason to be thankful that this chapter is in the Bible, because, as the report of a conflict in the Church, it provides us with an answer to all sorts of questions, a directive in all kinds of uncertainties. For there is more talk nowadays about conflict in the Church (in Germany and elsewhere) than there has been for many years.

What causes a conflict in the Church? We are told here that it arises because in the Church there emerge people with the best intentions and Christian zeal who no longer understand aright the grace of the Lord Jesus Christ (v. 11) in its unique redeeming power, who even fear and hate it and who extol and demand in its place or alongside it (as if anything could stand alongside it!) fulfilment of the Law as the condition for the salvation of man (vv. 1, 5 & 24). This means tempting God (v. 10) and leading men astray and overthrowing their souls (v. 24). And those who do this, act arbitrarily, because it is in no way decreed by the apostles (v. 24). We may well say that all conflict in the Church arises because people in the Church fight against grace and therefore, however pious or clever their intentions, cut themselves loose from the commands of the apostles. When this occurs, conflict is present.

What happens then? There is no help for it, a struggle has to develop, a struggle against these people (vv. 2 & 7). Paul and Barnabas, who took seriously the belief and knowledge that we are saved by Jesus Christ alone and in no way by our fulfilling of the Law, were unable to give way to those people for the sake of, say, peace and love. There are quarrels over power, possession, honour, influence, when one cannot give way too quickly. But where right and truth are attacked, it

[1] Published in *Leben und Glauben*, July 10, 1937.

would be acting against God, and against love and peace as well, to spare oneself the struggle or to wish to end it even one hour too soon. But there is no higher right and no greater truth than the free grace of Jesus Christ. The Church would be dead if a fight did not flare up within her against all enemies of this free grace.

Who or what will judge in this conflict? We read that the Christians from Antioch turned to the apostles in Jerusalem and that the apostles arbitrated in the conflict (vv. 2, 6, 22 & 23). Peter (vv. 7–11) and James (vv. 13–21) spoke, and by their speaking they let the prophets speak (vv. 15–17). Thus, when there is conflict in the Church, it is not as if there were no higher judge over and above the headstrong contenders. When there is strife in the Church, there is no reason at all for thinking that everybody may be right or perhaps nobody, and that the best course will doubtless be to break off the conflict. No, in the Church there is a judge. The judge alone may end the conflict. And the judge was then and is still today the Word of the apostles and prophets, who for this reason are called the foundation of the Church in Eph. 2: 20. They were and are the witnesses whom Jesus Christ has appointed for Himself. They knew what right and truth are, and in their Word, and thus in the Holy Scriptures, the contestants in the Church can and must be able to hear the right and the truth unmistakably at all times.

And what was their decision? We hear it in the words of Peter and James and in the letter which the apostles sent jointly to the community of Antioch (vv. 23–29). The conflict in the Church can be settled through the Word of the apostles, based on the Word of the prophets, which is the Word of God Himself, only by the joyful acknowledgement of what nothing but wrong and lying can deny—the free grace of Jesus Christ as the sole condition of life and blessedness for all men. This judgment then reduces them all to silence (vv. 12–13). In such conflicts this will always be the only judgment to be expected from this judge. By this judgment the unity of the Church is restored. By no other! Any other judgment would betray itself as that of some other, false judge and would be unable to settle the conflict. But this judgment has also the sanction of practice, of life: Where free grace is preached, there the Church is alive, for there God Himself is at work in this Word, visible in genuine conversions, in signs and miracles (vv. 3, 4, 12). It is therefore worth while (if one may ask at all in this context what is worth while) for the Church to submit itself to this judgment. She has reason to do so willingly.

Who is put in the right? Remarkably enough, none of the participants is placed completely in the right, not even those who were and are right, and so not even those who proclaim free grace. "That no flesh should glory in his presence" (1 Cor. 1: 29). When the Word of God has been spoken and heard, when the decision has been taken against all and every righteousness of works and arbitrariness, then love reminds us that we can and must admit that no-one in the Church has the right to cause offence to others, and that therefore, not for the sake of salvation but rather in complete freedom, we can be bidden to keep to the Law (vv. 20 & 29). So we must make concessions? No, no concessions! But precisely when the Church is completely firm on the substance, she will be able and will have to be quite flexible on the form.

And the end of the conflict? Read the chapter again and you will not fail to see that, despite the account of all sorts of bitterness which occurred then, something like a great joy lies over it. The conflict could and had to be fought, could and had to be decided, and decided in just this way. We see that it cost all its participants something, until it reached this point. But there is no lamenting about this. We hear that the proclamation of Paul and Barnabas continued and was also taken up by others (v. 35). We do not, however, know what became of those people who wanted to resist right and truth in the Church. They are unimportant people. What is important is the fact that the banners of the King were carried forward in this affair. "Which when they read, they were full of consolation" (v. 31). The word "consolation" in the Bible has always the sense of "exhortation" too. May this chapter also serve our Church and all of us who belong to her as consolation and exhortation!

II

THE CHURCH'S OPPOSITION 1933[1]

FUNDAMENTALS

1. Our protest is directed against the teaching of the German-Christians, represented by the government of the German Church, because it is false doctrine and has become the prevailing teaching in the Church through usurpation.

2. Because the doctrine and attitude of the German-Christians is nothing but a particularly vigorous result of the entire neo-protestant development since 1700, our protest is directed against a spreading and existent corruption of the whole evangelical Church.

3. Our protest against the false doctrine of the German-Christians cannot begin only at the "Aryan paragraph",[2] at the rejection of the Old Testament, at the Arianism of the German-Christian Christology, at the naturalism and Pelagianism of the German-Christian doctrines of justification and sanctification, at the idolizing of the state in German-Christian ethics. It must be directed fundamentally against the fact (which is the source of all individual errors) that, beside the Holy Scriptures as the unique source of revelation, the German-Christians affirm the German nationhood, its history and its contemporary political situation as a second source of revelation, and thereby betray themselves to be believers in "another God."

4. Our protest against the usurpation of the German-Christians cannot begin only with the cause of suspensions[3] and similar isolated interferences by the German-Christian Church governments. It must deny the legality of these Church governments as such in view of the events of June 24[4], of the Church elections of July 23[5], of the setting-

---

[1] Published in *Lutherfeier* (Luther Celebrations). Theol. Ex. h.4. 1933. pp. 20ff.
[2] That section in the German (*i.e.* National Socialist) Constitution by which Jews were debarred from citizenship.
[3] *i.e.* from office in the church.
[4] When Jäger was appointed by the state as Commissioner for Prussian Churches.
[5] The date of the Evangelical church elections.

up and also of the resolutions of the synods in August and September.[1]

5. Our protest must, in each single action, keep the nature and the extent of the Church's sickness in mind. It can, whether on individual points or as a whole, only be raised meaningfully, seriously and forcibly when we are clear and united about the nature and extent of this sickness and when, therefore, we wish to fight it in its nature and as a whole.

6. Whoever is of "another opinion" in any one of these five points himself belongs to the German-Christians and should not be permitted to disturb a serious opposition by the Church any longer.

[1] I cannot find that any Synod was held in August 1933. On September 5, however, the Prussian Church held a General Synod, and on September 21, the first National Synod was held at Wittenberg. For an account of both these Synods, see Duncan-Jones, pp. 50-51.

III

ON THE SITUATION 1933-34[1]

I

.... At the same time (the end of October, 1933) I turned down the offer of a seat on the newly-formed theological committee in the State Church government and terminated my membership of the theological examining body in the Rhine Consistory. I am divulging this information here in order to elucidate my opinion of the present situation in the Church. In view of the conception of Gospel and Church held by present Church governments (identical with that of the "German-Christians") and in view of the manner in which these governing bodies came to power by the elections of July 23 and then in the synods created by these elections (for Prussia we must add: in view of the resolutions of the general synod of September 6, 1933, especially of the "Church law concerning the proportions of power of ministers and Church officials")—in view of all this, we must regard the present position of the German Evangelical Church as a public emergency and treat it as such. The synodical element in Church government (in the narrower sense) has ceased to be a court to which we may listen in ministerial matters and in whose ministerial responsibility we may participate. Co-operation with this Church government, even if it may occasionally seem a practical advantage, implies fundamental recognition of the heresy that has infiltrated and of the usurpation that has taken place. But neither must be recognized under any circumstances and under any guise, if the Church, now seriously ill, is ever to be cured. Therefore any co-operation with the present Church government must also be regarded as finally unpractical. We can co-operate in the Church for the time being only in the sphere of the parishes, of parochial offices, and of theology, still free in doctrine and study. Here indeed it is our duty to co-operate as before. I regard talk of leaving the Church and of a free Church as irresponsible, so long as this sphere of activity is

[1] From the Foreword to *Reformation als Entscheidung* (Reformation as Decision).
Theol. Ex. h. 3. 1933, p. 3f.

not taken from us by a higher power. Let each man rather see to it that he fills his place in this sphere, as long as he has it, "unflaggingly and joyfully", as I suggested at the end of this lecture. "He that believeth shall not run away" (Is. 28: 16). Or according to the other translation of this verse: "He that believeth on him shall not be confounded".

Bonn, November 22, 1933.

II[1]

. . . . When I attended the meeting of the leaders of the Pastors' Emergency League, I found it moved and concerned more passionately over the possibility of an ecclesiastical and political exploitation of the situation created by the scandal of the Sports-palace[2] and by a few newly-pronounced suspensions and less passionately over the fundamental reflection demanded on that important day than behoves the good management of the Church's opposition today.

My great anxiety is that the opposition might prove under these circumstances to be as little equal to the exceptional danger of the present moment as it was last summer. And that precisely when all sorts of political successes should be coming its way! The government of the State Church and even the State administration of the German-Christians reacted promptly enough to that scandal by expelling the one among its accomplices who was primarily responsible for the mischief of that evening. In this way they have suddenly set themselves up as guardians of the need for "Bible and confession." The suspensions already pronounced were suspended. And even the Aryan-paragraph introduced with due legality by Bishop Müller in Prussia has, as a precaution, been put in cold storage for the time being by State-bishop Müller, his superior. In spite of everything that excellent theologians from north and south had already discovered and expressed to justify it! You see, another course of action *was* open!

Will the opposition ever understand that, in the crisis in which we are placed, nothing, absolutely nothing will be changed by all that? There was really no sense in the sudden attack on the German-Christians on November 15[3], as if only now, with the extravagances of Herr Krause, had the mystery of evil come to light. Of course the government of the

[1] From the Foreword to *Lutherfeier*. Theol. Ex. h. 4. 1933, pp. 3–7.
[2] The notorious public meeting in Berlin on Nov. 13, 1933, when Krause demanded the jettisoning of the Old Testament.
[3] *i.e.* because of the extravagances of the Sports-palace meeting.

State Church and the supposedly better members of the German-Christians were both forced and able to shake off this gentleman and even ignore the solemnly formed "resolution" of that meeting at the Sports-palace. Of course under the pressure of the painful situation which had developed they were forced and able to make those other concessions. There was no mention of the fact that such threads got in their way and that they could not set them aside. All this was possible because the substance of the German-Christian movement was in no way touched by it.

For exactly this reason there would now be no sense in wanting to argue from their concessions a serious change in the nature, position and character of the German-Christians, or of the governments of the German-Christian Church. So long as the false statement of their teaching (which indisputably governs the whole literature of the German-Christians (including the speeches of the State-bishop himself), and so long as the injustice, by which (on June 24, July 23, and afterwards) they came into possession of power in the Church; so long as these are not questioned comprehensively and honestly, it is of no avail if they should want to champion the supremacy of Scripture and the doctrine of justification as well, it is of no avail even if the wretched Aryan-paragraph tomorrow disappeared completely through the trap-door. And indeed, even a complete "Tannenberg"[1] of the German-Christians, even a hundred per cent political victory in the Church by the opposition, would be of no avail, if the opposition did not then understand the need to take hold of the roots of the malady in our Church, which has only broken out amongst the German-Christians, but which existed before them and is not now confined to them. Or contrariwise, the very formation of a free Church without clarification of the basic questions could be of no avail to us. It would have to be described as a downright national disaster if perhaps one neo-protestant hierarchy were to be replaced only by another of a somewhat lighter shade!

I know what I am talking about, for in those Berlin "days" I found absolutely everything that was troubling me in the summer about the then "Young Reformation Movement"[2] confirmed in an alarming

---

[1] *i.e.* overwhelming victory.

[2] A group which stood for the confessions of the Reformation in opposition to the German-Christians and also to the fusion of the Lutheran and Reformed Churches.

fashion. I am quite simply afraid that far from all of the three thousand[1] (with which number I cannot help thinking of Judges 7: 1—8) will understand that in face of the greater caution now practised in public we must not in the least think we have reached a decisive point, but that, if all is not to have been in vain, our opposition must rather go further and be fundamentally directed against the ecclesiastical and theological system of neo-protestantism in general, which is certainly not incorporated only in the German-Christians. I fear that many of those whose opposition to the German-Christians as such is meant sincerely and honestly do not understand that. Not to mention that they will decide to act as if they did not! To act separately from the German-Christian (but indeed not primarily and not only the German-Christian) substance of the error which has forced its way into the Church and now become obvious! But how shall anyone who is unaware of this substance and of the need to be rid of it (whether he belongs to the German-Christians or their opponents and however loudly he may talk of the much appealed to "substance of the Church") how shall he today have anything really useful to say, and know of anything really useful to do?

Because of the latest events, we are confronted by the irremediable danger that the conflict between neo-protestantism and its Reformation origins, which has become visible in this year's ecclesiastical trouble (a conflict which the German Evangelical Church might perhaps be called to wage today as the honourable representative to a certain extent of all other Churches) might once again not be decided, but rather be lamentably neutralized, perhaps be turned once again into a harmless source of argument between different theological schools. That the poison, accumulated and ripe for extraction, might spread out again and return to the circulation of the entire body. That those supposedly better members of the German-Christian Church and all those circles of the opposition who till now have indeed fought but not properly (*i.e.* not fundamentally), might find themselves in bad straits under the leadership of the governing bodies of the Church. That the result of all this year's pains and worries might be a new Church—of an undecided neo-protestant *via media*. This danger is really worse than all the dangers which may threaten us from the particular system of the German-Christians, a system condemned sooner or later to certain ruin.

In face of this danger the point cannot be made too urgently: the

[1] The Pastors' Emergency League originally consisted of 3,000 members.

question which is posed by the intrusion of the German-Christians (and also by the Luther celebrations, of all things!) implies an offer of unprecedented range made to the German Evangelical Church. The German-Christian defection and the threatening new *via media* following the partial treaty with it are not the only possibilities which stand before the German Evangelical Church today. As truly as she can hear today what the Church is, and as truly as she is the Church of Luther! Considering the German-Christians, she could finally be terrified at what has become of her, and, reflecting on Luther's Church, she could know herself to be called to what she has nevertheless not ceased to be. She could arise and turn round in her spiritual centre: from the ideologies to the simple, hard, glad truth of which she was born. She could once again become a holy Church, to the salvation of the German people—and perhaps also as the bearer of the light for other peoples.

For this to happen, not only would the German-Christians have to be driven from the field, but also and precisely the opposing three thousand would have to be freed from Saul's armour, from the continually too historical, philosophical, political, tactical and ostensibly (only ostensibly!) practical thinking, in which they have grown all too similar to the German-Christians and have failed to become their real enemy. But even if only thirty, only three, were in a position to do this, it would not be in vain, the turning point would be there, the offer made to us would be accepted. Where the Word of God is once again simply heard and preached, there is the holy Church. I greet these thirty or three, and I have grounds for pointing out to the others that there are innumerable non-theologians in Germany even today who understand all this very well and who rightly wait for the theologians also finally to understand it better.

What shall we do? One thing, and one only.

> "Let each turn his eyes right round
> Straight towards Jerusalem!"

In all weakness and foolishness and perversity, which no single one of us will avoid, but "straight" and "right round"! Where that happens, everything has happened. Where not, nothing has happened.

Bonn, November 19, 1933.

III[1]

.... The Evangelical Church affairs in Germany have developed fast

[1] From the Foreword to *Die Kirche Jesu Christi* (The church of Jesus Christ). Theol. Ex. h. 5. 1933, pp. 4–7.

since I wrote the Foreword to Number 4. Herr Krause's speech in the Sports-palace and the applause of his 19,999 has set off a continually widening circle of waves. The affair of the so widely discussed and greatly cultivated Mission to the People with which the German-Christians, and along with them the new church, thought they would prove their right to exist, has retired into the background again after its somewhat unhappy beginning. The solemn institution of the State-bishop, planned for the first Sunday in Advent, has not taken place. By resigning his post of "patron" of the German-Christians and recommending a similar neutrality to his ministers and the collective government of the Church, the State-bishop seemed to separate himself at once from those who had engineered his rise. The leading figure of the German-Christians, Bishop Hossenfelder, disappeared (after he had proved—too late!—that he too could act differently) not indeed from the "State administration", but at any rate from the Church's government.

And now something like a catastrophe seemed suddenly and strangely to break upon the German-Christians themselves. One man's hand was lifted against another. While one faction in the ranks of the Faith Movement[1] stood up for Herr Krause and accused Bishop Hossenfelder[2] of all people of an obsolete dogmatism, the other faction waxed enthusiastic over the energetic way in which the State Church's government and management had proceeded against the "heresy". Yet another group, amongst them many German-Christians, suddenly found the whole thing sinister. Some simply offered actual opposition to what had been till then the Faith Movement by attaching themselves, as if they had never had any other intentions, to the declarations of protest and confession (which are suddenly falling like hail-stones), against Krause's leadership, and against the Hossenfelder régime, or even by playing a leading part in them. Again others have "declared themselves independent of the State management," a proceeding which is hardly clear as crystal and also not exactly in character. Dramatic arguments arose between Hossenfelder and Professors Fezer, Rückert and Weiser of Tübingen, in which the American Dr. Frank Buchman (the founder and leader of the Oxford Group Movement—how did he come to be aboard this galley?) played a rôle not known in detail, and which ended

---

[1] The full title of the German-Christian Movement was *Glaubensbewegung Deutscher Christen* (Faith Movement of German Christians).
[2] The leader of the German-Christians until Kinder supplanted him.

after much coming and going with the voluntary departure of the professors from the Faith Movement.

But much use seems to have been made in other quarters, too, of the possibility of retiring from the movement as simply as from the first and best union. In Württemberg, but according to all reports here in the West too, genuine emigrations do really seem to have taken place. The Bavarians (it is not yet clear what they really intended) have pledged loyalty to their Bishop in regard to the confusions in North Germany. In short, many now suddenly wished that they had not been quite so sure of themselves! But, if the report is true, the three thousand members of the Pastors' Emergency League mentioned in my previous Foreword have at the same time swollen to seven thousand. Small cause, large effects!

Whether all this spells the end of the German-Christians, who not long ago were still forging ahead so strongly, it is not possible to say at the moment, nor is it very important. I can only repeat myself here: their spears were and are hollow, and sooner or later this badly undertaken affair will lead to a bad ending. But we are not concerned with the German-Christians, but rather with our Evangelical Church, in whose precincts and bosom all this has happened, and happened in such a way that all of us, whether we belong to the German-Christians now, or used to, or even if we are in the opposition, have cause to be ashamed of ourselves before God and the angels, that such a thing could happen.

There was so little understanding among us that it needed the crude paganism of Herr Krause to unleash the storm of an indignation which, had it been genuine, would have broken out last June at the latest. This indignation was so weak that, till now, it has resulted only in a few proposed rearrangements of officials, but in no way in a shaking of the theological and ecclesiastical system under which we stand. And so very shallow, that at its climax it was no more than a struggle against Hossenfelder and for the second (not better!) form of the German-Christian "Right lines". Many hundreds of pastors seem to have been so unaware of what they were doing last summer when, at the head of their parishes, they allied themselves to the German-Christians, that they were able as quickly to revoke the barely pledged support for the direction of their "movement" (their "Faith Movement"), so as to-morrow—who knows?—to fall prey to some other "movement". Brave "decisions" and orthodox confessions of faith are to be had so cheaply that the Churches are suddenly echoing with them; whereas in the summer, when everything was at stake, silence reigned or nearly everyone howled with the wolves. And we, who are now blessed with so many "bishops", are so bereft of any genuine, unambiguous, dependable leadership that one may well ask whether the Evangelical Church has ever to such an extent been a flock without a shepherd.

Really, there is no cause for triumph or even partial composure in view of the events which lie behind us. They have brought us no alleviation. They have shown us (and indeed I hold myself partially responsible for this, after having worked in this Church for twelve years) how little faith, love and hope is alive among us.

If this turns out to be the end of the German-Christians, it may well be said: *Afflavit Deus et dissipati sunt!* But then (and how much more, if the end of the matter has not yet been reached) we would all have to make together a completely new start with determination and vigilance. It will not be achieved with a Deuteronomic reform of the Temple. We need to be converted. What is in store for us could be worse than what has already happened. . . .

Bonn, December 11, 1933.

IV[1]

The readers of this booklet know my view: conversion, spiritual consolidation, opposition to the chronic, crawling, latent outside control are necessary if we are not to be threatened immediately by new and most grave dangers. The real problem which confronts us today (beside the question of how, if God will, we can be rid of the nuisance of the German-Christians) lies in the existence of the Protestant modernism (only partially coincidental with ecclesiastical and theological "liberalism"), which has broken out among the German-Christians. I am glad that this view, expressed in article I of the "declaration", has achieved a certain value in the Church through the resolution of the Synod of Barmen.[2] It is to be expected that I (and let us hope others too) will have to return to this greater historical relationship of the present crisis with a *Ceterum censeo*.

[1] From the Foreword to *Gottes Wille und unsere Wünsche* (God's Will and our Wishes). Theol. Ex. h. 7, 1934, pp. 4–8.
[2] Not the famous Synod of Barmen, May 29–31, 1934, but an earlier one, held Jan. 3–4, 1934. It was distinguished from the *First Confessional Synod of the German Evangelical Church in Barmen* by being confined to the Reformed Church. For its confession of Faith (composed by Barth) see A. Keller: *Religion and the European Mind* (London, 1934) pp.178ff.

I hope I shall not be misunderstood, therefore, if I once again insist that we have cause, in, with and under all the sighing forced from us, to be glad and grateful at the sight of what has happened and been achieved, and more, what may happen again. I would not have believed it (humanly speaking) in the past years, but it is now manifestly the case: two or more centuries of the gravest theological and Church political devastation and the heaviest external pressure of the present day have not had such effect that men can do today what they like with the Evangelical Church, this poor maiden. But suddenly there were, and still are, in existence again—confession and (with all the only too comprehensible confusion and in all the admitted questionability of the insights and motives) the confessors as well. But let each man ask himself and others (this cannot be asked too much) how genuine, how pure, how strong this confession is. No-one has ultimately the competence and right to the heart-searching thesis that it is in general false, impure and weak. It is impossible to deny in faith today that, whatever may be the case with confessors, confession itself was and is very much in the picture. And then one may well stand in the much acclaimed "sphere of the Church" with a grim face, but in no way with a sour, worried face. Wherever one believes it (*credo unam sanctam catholicam et apostolicam ecclesiam*) there the Church *is* and there one has cause to be joyful.

The other thing I would like to say in introduction is this: the Barmen Declaration is first of all a declaration of German parishes of the *Reformed* confession. But it was in my mind to speak in the title of the "German *Evangelical* Church of today". Moreover, I have been able to win over my Reformed brethren (although it was not easy for many of them) to agree wholeheartedly to Article 1 § 3 of this Declaration[1], and for the rest (without at all sacrificing anything of the Reformed "heritage and responsibility" of these synods, but rather in continuation of the best Reformed tradition) I think I have said everything in such a way that stalwart Lutherans, without on their part sacrificing anything, could speak with us, although of course their spontaneous confession would assume a different shape from ours. I believe that in this way and no other can one and *must* one confess in the German Evangelical Church today. Lutherans and Reformed cannot and must not confess

[1] Article 1 § 3 acknowledged "the essential unity of the faith, love and hope, of the proclamation through preaching and sacrament, of the confession and the task of "the one German Evangelical Church" irrespective of the fact that it consisted of Lutheran, Reformed and "United" Churches.

today in opposition, but rather in unison as evangelical-Lutherans and evangelical-Reformed. I have never been a friend of the so-called "Union"[1] of the nineteenth century, nor am I one today. It was born, if appearances are not deceptive, not from a common confession, but from the lack of understanding and confession which had become acute among Lutherans and Reformed alike. Its history in the last hundred years was therefore destined to be a stumbling-block, and this in fact has happened. This gives its specific pathos something of falseness.

The error which has broken out today in the theology and Church politics of the German-Christians originated neither in the school of Luther nor of Calvin, but is rather (Schleiermacher, R. Rothe, W. Beyschlag might be named among its particular fathers) the typical error of the final phase of that "Union" of the nineteenth century. It violates the Lutheran as well as the Reformed confession. For precisely this reason Lutherans and Reformed are summoned (wherever their particular ways may stem from and lead to) to an agreement on the faith today. Luther's hymn "Uphold us, Lord, with Thy Word" has been a particular comfort at these times to many Lutherans and Reformed alike. "With Thy Word" it runs—not: with our "proceedings" which we must take so seriously! And moreover: "Prove Thy strength, Lord Jesus Christ"—not: the good historical right of our confessional separated existence! And moreover: "Protect Thy poor Christendom" —not: Lutheranism or the Reformed tradition! And moreover: "God, the holy Ghost, thou worthy comforter, give thy people *one* disposition on earth"—not: preserve for one his Low-Saxon and for another his Low-Rhenish stubbornness! I do indeed take the differences between Lutherans and Reformed seriously; but, because I take them seriously, I cannot see how far we *today* can be summoned to confess to them otherwise than in the agreement of faith.

Conflict in the Church today is not centred on the Lord's Supper but on the first commandment and it is on this question that we have to "confess" today. In the face of our distress and task the Church of the fathers must retire; that is, she must become a still serious, but no longer dividing, no longer splitting, counterpart of the theological school. Place the already mentioned eight articles of the Lutheran H. Vogel and our Barmen Declaration side by side and ask yourself: although, or precisely because, the particular confessional "heritage and responsibility" receives its due meed in both cases, is such an agreement not

[1] Between Lutherans and Reformed, under Friedrich Wilhelm III of Prussia from 1817 onwards.

possible and is it, in face of the common enemy today, not plain necessary? Read also the just published first number in the series produced by Hans Asmussen, Fritz Collatz and Rudolf Jaeger called "The Community-Church" and ask yourself whether, in view of the mutual contact afforded by the closeness of the Lutheran and Reformed interpretation of the *form* of the Church, one can talk even in this sphere of an irremediable antagonism.

It is definitely not true (only an irresponsible journalism or an equally irresponsible archaism can assert it) that we are called upon today to play Luther and Calvin off against each other—today when the *sola fide* is as important as the *soli deo gloria* in the face of justification by works. It is not true that the theologumenon of the identity of God's Law with the so-called orders of creation or the theologumenon of the authoritative bishop are genuinely and essentially Lutheran teachings. Nor again is it true that Calvinism must be suspected of rationalism just because a goodly injection of iron into the blood stream was more important to it than the mysteries of this blood which may perhaps be emphasized elsewhere.

I am not concerned here with the theological and Church-political agreements which will have to come some day, if we do not want to have combined in the one "German Evangelical Church" in vain. But I am concerned with the credal presupposition of such an agreement. I would like to raise the question publicly: Has not this presupposition already become visible in the conflict forced upon us today for the truth and against error? Is it not worth while to say "yes" to it sincerely in the first place, so as then to consider from this standpoint theology and Church politics, which will certainly have to be considered, but in that case perhaps more seriously and forcefully than before? Their numerical superiority ought on no account to stop the Lutherans hearing our question today, if we ask them to. However few there may be of us, they are not alone in the German Evangelical Church. The question about evangelical agreement is set before them, and not by us alone; the only thing is whether they want to have this question placed aright before themselves. . . .

Bonn, January 26, 1934.

V[1]

Since the appearance of my previous writing in this series there has

---

[1] From the Foreword to *Offenbarung, Kirche, Theologie* (Revelation, Church, Theology). Theol. Ex. h. 9, 1934, pp. 3–13.

been plenty of movement and excitement in the sphere of German Church history and many have been surprised that I have kept silence for so long. But what was there to say about the fact that the government of the State Church has once again taken Müller under its wing, when his days already seemed numbered at the beginning of the year, and has given powerful proof of its existence by enactment of the law and by suspensions, ignoring all written and unwritten Church law?

We always had to allow for the possibility that the evil, even merely in its external and tangible form, would not be so quickly exhausted as seemed likely for a while. And also that even in the camp of their friends, a few are quietly and secretly aware that the kind of proof of existence now provided by the German-Christian powers cannot suffice in the long run, that a Church government with only the authority of actual possession and power will not succeed, that Church government needs intellectual and spiritual authority, something which this Church government utterly and completely lacks. What was there to say to the fact that at the end of January the so-called leaders of the Church should once again be confounded in a situation in which they should have been thinking simply of the Church instead of trivialities (the classic example was the fact that the whole system of bishops has now come to nothing) and that in their train many lesser people who had just taken a bit of courage should again become timid and subservient?

No-one who met those men with personal trust for a while need be ashamed of the fact; but it is not surprising that they did not justify it then. In the sphere where the only fundamental principle is a complete lack of principles, we shall of necessity continually experience such surprises, even in the case of the most honest and trustworthy people, at a time when everything should depend on principles.

And when it became apparent that the situation was different from that of the summer of 1933; when the Pastors' Emergency League was certainly not "on its way out" and German Protestantism in no way "on its death-bed", as the Swiss papers were saying in March; when, rather, resistance (and indeed not only Church-political but also spiritual resistance) flamed up from every quarter; when one Free Confessional Synod followed another; when the parishes in the west really have, to a large extent, stood up and spoken; when the desired unanimity between Lutherans and Reformed has been largely realized in this affair (and not only in the west);—what is there to say to all this but that everyone who enquires closely and seriously about the Church today has greeted and accompanied these events with thankfulness and hope as faith-strengthening symptoms of a promising development? We have very many more signs that can confidently stand up to inspection than have the poor State bishops. All this can now be said after the event with a mixture of doubts and comprehension and joy. But now—how will it continue? how should it continue?

I have just finished reading Emanuel Hirsch's new book: "The present spiritual situation as mirrored in philosophy and theology."[1] No-one should fail to study it. In contrast to almost everything that I have read of the productions of the German-Christian camp, it is a well-considered and also readably and interestingly written book, which has said, better than any previous book, the best that can be said for the German-Christian cause. We can and must praise it too for the fact that its author, in contrast to many of his fellow-believers, has, with what he declared today, remained in line with what he has always meant, intended and maintained. If anyone is genuine and has the right to speak in this affair, it is Emanuel Hirsch. This is what makes it so clear and certain that, and why, faced with this book, we must say No, No, and once again No, to this matter. Our denial is as unarguable as Hirsch's introduction and establishment of the subject in its basic theme.

This basic theme consists in the hypothesis that the present spiritual situation (*i.e.* the so-called "German hour") is to be "interpreted" as a "meeting with God". Hirsch wants to build the Church on this rock and this rock only. It is from this viewpoint that he construes her preservation, her renovation, her task. His view of history is centered on this. The spirits are divided here for him. Here the worth, or lack of it, of all philosophy and theology is decided according to him. Within the framework of the recognition of this thesis he will speak of everything or a great deal; but, outside this framework, of nothing at all. Into the reality affirmed in this thesis, theology and the Church have to weave themselves, to let themselves be woven, to be woven together with it.

In terms of this book a confession of faith would definitely have to begin with the avowal that God, that Jesus Christ, is the "Lord of history" in the special sense of what appeared on the scene in 1933 with, according to Hirsch, the assumption and the power of the final,

[1] *Die gegenwärtige geistige Lage im Spiegel philosophischer und theologischer Besinnung.* (Göttingen, 1934).

deepest historical dominance, asking searching questions and demanding answers. Of course, Hirsch knows also that Christianity is not to be understood as only a force of history, a racial ordinance and a general spirituality; but as the rest of its qualities he can only name questioning of the conscience, inward relationship with God, the mystery of faith. What wonder then if, in this limited antithesis, the first side, and with it the significance of the "German hour" as salvation and revelation, is so predominant in each and every connection in his book that anyone who cannot concur in this great interpretation can, under the gravest suspicion of not knowing what decision is, ultimately only let himself be banished as an exoteric "to silence". "If we in theology and Church are too small for His hour, if we cannot, by surrendering all the prejudice stemming from the past and all our need for assurance and security, risk ourselves to the inrushing 'new', to our own folk in its living movement, then we are cast out. There is no middle way; only the Either—Or. No man who puts his hand to the plough and looks back is fit for the kingdom of God. Nor can the new Germany use such a one." (p. 132f.).

In fact, in Hirsch there is lacking all and every "assurance and security" whether from biblical exegesis, whether from connection with Church tradition. In fact, everything is not only basically, but also manifestly, "risk"; that is, free speculation or brooding, a speculation into which "the Gospel" and Luther are drawn at particular points, in which they have their very important and worthy place, yet speculation, arbitrary experiment, preaching on a theme and without a text (it might be that one would wish to take as a text the "hour" experienced by Hirsch), a theologically valueless "Kairos philosophy," which indeed clears out all the theological elements like that of his religio-social antipodes, Paul Tillich. And it is this which, as the basic thesis not only of Hirsch's book but also of the teaching and behaviour of Müller's Church government and of the German-Christians in general, is their basic error. For, however cleverly and comprehensively, however piously and Christianly, it may be intended and expressed, it is pure fanaticism compared to everything that has hitherto been so described in Church history (I have no intention at all of abandoning this "prejudice")—fanaticism which, if it were to prevail, would cause the dissolution of the evangelical Church and its deserved surrender to the Pope, who can do all this so much better.

Against this error must be set the Christian centre, which is the theoretical and practical, inward and outward basis of the Church, and the object of theology—the Word of God, or Jesus Christ, crucified and risen, stands as Lord, as Creator, as Reconciler, as Redeemer, over and above that confused separation and integration of Germanism and personal Christianity, with which alone their view is concerned.

This hour certainly does not coincide with an arbitrarily chosen and interpreted hour of Christian and German history; and the boundary which He sets us certainly does not coincide with an arbitrarily indicated moment of Christian and German truth. But this hour is His own hour and this boundary is His own boundary. Before Him the weaving and being woven are of no account. Before Him only faith and obedience are of value. From Him we are asked time and again with reference to the supposedly clearly recognized "Lord of history" whether perhaps we have not simply imagined a demon. And whatever we imagined will certainly always turn out to have been the demon. For from Him—through and in Himself, so that He is and remains the Lord—comes the justification and sanctification of the sinner and not such a favouring of the man who dares as to make him into a little Lord and master. He is indeed with us every day until the end of the world, but not in such a way that He would be swallowed up by our days and the bold grasping which is the significance of our days, not in such a way that we should have the mission and authority to interpret our days as we like, so as then to give His holy name confidently to the thing our interpretation has created. It is enough and more than enough if we with our daring, grasping and interpreting in large and small things, may walk before Him in fear and joy, praying, thanking and praising, because we are accepted in grace—and therefore truly in no respect at a desolate distance from Him, but also in no respect as His Privy Councillors and co-regents who could with their venturing, grasping and interpreting announce and decree where, what and how His reality and His will are here and now.

If in the one holy catholic Church anything has to be relegated "to silence", it is the free private opinion (be it that of one individual or of countless people), which would make us seek and honour God as "Lord of history" today here and tomorrow there, this man in this way and that man in that. The Church is there, and only there, where God is sought as and where He wants to be sought, but that means along with the witnesses, in the remembrance, investigation, expositon and application of that message of the Old and New Testament which alone established the Church and which alone can uphold it and will and shall continually renew it quite alone.

Care has been taken and will always be taken to ensure that even this search for God will be always a human and all too human thing, that it will continue completely in the sphere of the world and under the influences of all sorts of historical hours and will bear such things inside itself. It can and shall therefore be and remain this quite definite search, bound to the Scripture, which constitutes and distinguishes the Church as Church. It must nevertheless not become an arbitrary search in that sphere and in these hours. The Church would not only have to surrender herself but to deny her mission and service, indeed to betray her Lord, if she wanted to change over to proclaiming such an arbitrarily sought and found thing as "God", whom she should call upon, whose goodness and severity she should publish abroad, whose name she should love and praise. The Church, the German evangelical Church no less, lives on the one Word of God, from which she is born, and on no second word alongside it. This it is which must be opposed to the Church government of Müller and to the German-Christians as a whole, as untiringly as they themselves seem for the time being to be tireless not only in saying the false opposite but also in proclaiming it and making it valid as the foundation of the Church with cunning and force, partly in the compelling tone of the propaganda of the popular speaker, partly in the sober and persuasive tone of the academic theologian, partly in the rough and organizing tone of the Churchman. Hirsch is quite right: "There is only the Either—Or."

Why am I saying this at precisely this moment? I am saying it at precisely this moment because in the question as to how matters will and shall continue after the events of the past three months, something or perhaps everything depends on whether and how this is understood —"There is only the Either—Or". Will it be understood now and in the future as clearly and basically as Hirsch sees it and as it must be formulated in contradiction to Hirsch by the other side? Or will it once again develop on one side or the other, or on both, into haziness, into clever but hazy blurrings and admixtures?

Before me lie two other important documents: State-bishop Müller's Good Friday message to the pastors and the "Letter to pastors and members of parishes on how peace may be won in the Church" by Pastor Friedrich von Bodelschwingh, published on February 15. There remains nothing for me than to admit that I counter both writings (although of course I can discern between the two spirits) materially with this question: Are their authors aware of the full seriousness of the decision before us and of the need to make it under all circumstances, or is a weakening of that seriousness taking place here and a disguising of that need, against which we cannot be warned too urgently at this precise moment?

In the case of the State-bishop's Good Friday message, this question can be unambiguously answered. It is downright shocking to see how unsuspectingly this man takes for granted (he calls it "unsparing objectivity"), and time and again assumes and declares, that the dogma of the salvation and revelation of 1933 is the yard-stick of everything, so that no connection between Scripture and Church seems to exist for him at all. And then he asks the pastors, "in the light of Christ crucified" whether they really think that, to be obedient to God, they have to be disobedient to him. And to speak as if only reasons like "pastoral timidity, scruples, uncertainty" or "Church-political need for excitement" and even more sinister situations and agitations could really be considered! On this basis then: peace, peace! "It is not a question of conflict between two administrations but of the maintenance of Church order."

That for a long time there have no longer been only two "administrations" but very nearly two separate Churches, and that it was his Church, the German-Christian Church, which necessitated the antagonism by proclaiming that new and false dogma and which, if that dogma does not disappear, has made the antagonism irremediable—this seems not to have been realized yet in Charlottenburg. And thus, in the classical manner, they cry peace where no peace is, nor can be, nor may be. Thus they recommend subjection to a "Church order" which consists of the declaration of the permanence of all Church disorder. Thus they want to administer a narcotic to the pastors with their talk of Christ crucified, just when the last of them should wake from his sleep and rise up at the memory of Good Friday and Easter.

One would think it unnecessary to have to speak out expressly and say that we are concerned here with an illicit blurring of the most necessary contradictions, that this voice is of course not to be heard. But one never quite knows where one stands. I have just heard of a large regional Church where, encouraged by the happenings in Westphalia, they wanted to rouse themselves at last to reflection and action and where, on this State-bishop's advice, a semi-retreat was then sounded just the same from the highest ecclesiastical position and throughout that Church.

So it really is necessary to say expressly: the German-Christian dogma is no less false because, if he is not in the mood to meet his opponents with much rougher words, it can please the State-bishop on occasion to keep to peace, forgiveness and the Cross—and one should not let oneself be deceived by the one or the other of his methods into thinking anything but that the Church is being attacked in its foundations by him and his followers, and that he must be resisted to his face in memory of Good Friday and Easter. As long as a declaration like this Good Friday message can make an impression and can dislodge leading men from the responsibility they have already entered upon, so long is the situation in the Church, despite all better impulses, still desperately bad.

It must certainly be assumed that the ecclesio-political content of this message (into which I will not go here) has sufficed to make it ineffective on the whole. But if the Church government had not been stricken with blindness in this respect, if it had had the cleverness to come out with an amnesty? Would her false dogma alone have sufficed to keep open the continually closing eyes of so many people? Would the devotional message of Good Friday not have won over the hearts of many for the curse of the Church, who theologically would have been ready at any moment not to be over-particular, for whom therefore that German-Christian dogma presents no decisive question? I am only asking. But truly: this question must be asked today because of the way countless people still think and feel.

In the case of Pastor von Bodelschwingh's circular, such an unambiguous position is naturally out of the question. But that is exactly the problem: Why can I not, as I really would like to, say "Yes" to this document as unambiguously as "No" to the other? There are many good words in it, words of personal pastoral exhortation, which everyone can certainly always make some use of and listen to, many ecclesiastical directives which deserve to be heard and taken to heart. And I fully realize that Pastor von Bodelschwingh for his part does not stand on the ground of the false dogma, and in accordance with his whole way of thinking belongs unquestionably with those whose will is different from that destructive will which has broken out among the German-Christians in our Church.

But where does he stand, and what exactly does he say? This is not clear to me from reading his manifesto and I must say, in view of his recognized position of leadership, it has remained painfully unclear. Why, apart from the things which are always true and worth hearing, does he not say on any single occasion what we are concerned with today and in which direction we must unambiguously face? Why does he, too, talk of the various "groups" and "camps" in the well-known

35

way in which one addresses conflicting brothers, so as not to increase further the existing tensions, but just to review the possibility of their finding an understanding with each other in a higher third position, though meanwhile listening to and learning from each other?

Can he then still believe that, for instance, Hirsch and I should listen to and learn from each other, as one could once upon a time expect, perhaps with some right, of a "Positive Theologian" and a "Liberal"? Are matters in the Church today not so dangerous that there should be inescapable responsibilities, that one should have to choose, and not only on one's own, but that every man should have to be called out and challenged to choose with Joshua and Elijah? Does the German-Christian dogma, apart from Bodelschwingh's charitable interpretation of it, entail no decisive question for him too? But if it does not, why does he not tell us from his superior insight, why it does not and to what extent? For if it is, for Hirsch and myself for instance, a decisive question, a question on whose decision according to both our views the Church stands or falls—what help to us then is any advice, any assurance that our contradictions will be overcome without compromise or insincerity "under the omnipotent power of the Word"? That would not only have to be assured, it would have to be theologically explained to us.

Or, in the last resort, is Bodelschwingh too of the opinion that no decision at all is involved in the theological question, in other words in the question of truth, and that there need be none; that the Church can recognize the source of her revelation just as well in the Scriptures alone as in the Scriptures *and* the "German hour," if only a hearing be given to the moral and practical request that he proposed and if everybody loved everybody else? Where should we stand if Bodelschwingh (I take good care not to ascribe it to him) should answer this last question in the affirmative? From what "beyond" of love, or—from which nineteenth century liberalism, would this affirmation come? But where do we stand if Bodelschwingh does not affirm this question and yet still talks as if this were no matter of an absolutely serious theological responsibility and decision, as if even today the Church needed only that certainly true and necessary exhortation? Here too I can only ask.

But I must ask, because with all due respect to Bodelschwingh, I really do not understand his intentions. And I must ask openly and urgently, because in Westphalia and elsewhere it will depend substantially on Bodelschwingh which path the now awakened Church resistance will or will not take. If it remains burdened with that theological indecision (as I wish for the moment neutrally to describe the attitude of his circular) then I should like to ask: What is the real aim of this resistance? From what last bitter necessity—if it is not a theological one—does it spring? With what sense and seriousness was confession made in Barmen, Berlin and Dortmund? For what cause have the disciplined pastors suffered? What have we all been fighting about for nearly a year now? And what is the courage, what the responsibility and what the faith with which we are steering towards the free Church of which there is more and more talk on all sides? Shall it, too, be a Church of theological indecision, in which one dogma stands peacefully beside its counter-dogma, at whose founding there will be as little decisive questioning after the truth as there was at the founding of the Prussian Union Church, whose demise we have now experienced with horror? Will open heresy issue from this new free Church as consistently as from that other one?

All that I can and will ask only, as it were, in brackets; for I know how many younger people will answer indignantly that they have no such intentions. But if they really and truly have no such intentions in the circles of the opposition, may we not ask such a spokesman and representative of the opposition as Bodelschwingh to speak out loudly and firmly and not to address those who already do so as a "camp", opposed to which there is another "camp", two camps between which one can, and indeed must, take up a position somewhere in the middle? If the promise under which we all think we see the Church opposition today is to be realized, must we not admit that the love of God and our neighbour which we have to practise in the German evangelical Church today consists in asking ourselves inexorably the theological question, the question of truth, the question "Scripture or 1933?", and in letting the decision come upon us without reservation?

Easter Day, April 1, 1934.

VI[1]

This time little need be said on the state of affairs in the Church. As we look back to the week after Easter, we must be thankful that the Church has a Good Shepherd, who always secretly shows and proves Himself as such especially when it is most obvious that all human

---

[1] From the Foreword to *Der gute Hirte* (The Good Shepherd). Theol. Ex. h. 10, 1934. pp. 3-5.

attempts at leadership in the Church are of no avail. But there is also reason for looking longingly around for the signs of this His secret governing: "Watcher, is the night soon gone?"

Müller's Church government has continued to experiment (or should and can this to-ing and fro-ing between Christian and political motives, this switch from sweetmeats to the whip, should and can an affair like the latest with the new "legal administrator"[1] be so described?) They experiment in such a way that it is almost tangibly clear how the right means to gain their evil ends continually occur to them either too late or not at all, and are replaced equally continually by all kinds of means by which they will achieve the opposite of their aim. It will and can not be the case that evil business can be carried through well, even only technically. Of course, we dare not think of how many of the weak and foolish, who are yet our brothers, up and down the country have been oppressed, lamed, warped, destroyed by this rule. The Church could not compromise herself more thoroughly than through these people, to whom we cannot even give the testimonial that, even though they had not done good, at least they had done wrong soundly. On the other hand, we can hardly fail to misunderstand that precisely in their unloveliness they are an instrument in a higher hand and must exercise a protective as well as a quickening function in the face of all the incompleteness, weakness, mediocrity and thoughtlessness, very much against that higher will, not to mention their own.

In view of this we must continually refrain from wishing on them too eagerly their long deserved downfall. Where should we have been, what sort of weak production would have come out of the evangelical Church at this time, if it had been allowed to slumber on in undisturbed continuity from the second into the third Reich, if these German-Christians and the Müller régime had not been prescribed for us with all its errors, outrages and shaming ludicrousness—prescribed just like a poisoned pill? So that at last people should once again ask, as they should do, about Scripture, confession, community, divine service, preaching, theology; so that at last people should be brought to the point of recollections, testings and reparations for old failings and omissions; so that the Church might learn to understand herself again as Church in German Protestantism—so that all this should occur, perhaps what has come to pass was necessary. The learned know that I am

---

[1] Jäger was appointed Müller's "legal administrator" on April 12, 1934. His office, ostensibly a sop to the opposition, was to distinguish between ecclesiastical and state politics.

here only repeating what the Church fathers said regularly whenever they reflected on the matter; why does God allow heresy and defection in the Church? Answer: so that the Church may learn to stand so much the more firmly and to know the truth completely afresh. They were right. Perhaps we still do not stand firmly enough and perhaps we have not yet sufficiently learnt the truth afresh for us not to need the German-Christian establishment yet awhile!

And if we are ever honourably rid of it, then (we must remember this continually) the real problems and cares will be just beginning. It will then have to become apparent whether in this time of acute trouble we have learnt anything in regard to the necessary edification of the community through the Word and in the Spirit, and whether we are willing permanently to submit to the discipline which this time has brought upon us. This time continually shows itself now to be a real time of need—not only in regard to the German-Christians but also to so much that happens and does not happen on the so-called "confessional fronts". "Oh, God, look down from heaven!" we may sigh: let us at last see things straightforwardly in the junctures and situations where time and time again we should like to be clever! Let theology at last become primary for us and Church politics only secondary, so that in this properly ordered relationship it may become good politics! Let us together at last think and want one thing, instead of always at heart something dual! Let those in the North and South at last become *dependable*—at least as dependable as men can be! Let us at last act as we have confessed! For otherwise what use are all our confessions and confessional fronts?

The peace which the Emergency League in Schleswig-Holstein made with the German-Christians and with their bishops to the accompaniment of a Whitsun hymn was a bad affair which we hope will not be imitated. And how seriously the so-called "Ulm declaration"[1] was really intended and could be intended by the people behind it, at least still remains to be seen. When they invoked the Holy Trinity there, would it not have been better to wait, at least until there had been more definite signs for unity in the Spirit, for the purity of the various purposes, for the certainty of their positions? A thick fog still continues to lie all over this landscape. And when

---

[1] The declaration of the Ulm Conference (April 22, 1934) not only attacked the State-bishop on the grounds of acting illegally, but also claimed, in effect, that the confessing Church was "the constitutional Evangelical Church of Germany".

we ask ourselves where and how the Church of Christ may come into the picture again here, we could well lose hope.

Looking to the one Good Shepherd, who always makes good what we do badly, may be even more necessary in the future than in the past and at present.

Bonn. May 4, 1934.

IV

THE CONFESSING CHURCH
IN NATIONAL SOCIALIST GERMANY[1]

WHEN NATIONAL SOCIALISM gained its long desired or feared power
in Germany in the spring of 1933, it proved immediately to be a tyranny
of previously unheard of dimensions, partly on account of the inward
and outward condition of the German people since the World War,
partly by virtue of the power of propaganda in its ideas, symbols
and formations, partly by virtue of the unusually energetic method
of government which it used. There was at once no sphere of life on
which it did not make demands and from which it would not have
claimed practical response to its demands pretty quickly. The political
parties, commerce, administration and justice, art, the universities,
the schools and youth education in its widest sense, the press, public
and private welfare, and countless people who had been regarded
previously as "characters" have submitted to its demands, because
they had to and could do. The whole proud heritage of the eighteenth
and nineteenth centuries proved incapable of resistance, obviously
because it contained nothing that *had* to resist and *could* not give way.

Who would have expected that there would have been anything
different to say about the evangelical Church, which has become in
our time so weak in itself and of so little public significance? Yet in the
evangelical Church there has come about, meagrely, painfully, un-
surely, but undeniably, a rediscovery and an open confession of a
Christian nature which, being subject to no earthly power, did not let
itself be geared to the National Socialists, and for the sake of which,
therefore, people had to swim against the stream, for better or worse.

The questions before which the evangelical Church was placed, as
it were overnight, in the spring of 1933 were these: Whether it was
possible to adopt, as it were, into the Christian faith the ideas of National
Socialism (blood, race, nationality, the soil, leadership etc.) which had
suddenly won the day and were being proclaimed in all the streets
with the most popular persuasiveness and at the same time with the

[1] *Zwingli-Kalender*, 1936. Written summer 1935.

highest authority, and therefore to let these ideas become authoritative also for the preaching, teaching and organization of the Church. Whether the event of the National Socialist revolution was to be regarded and honoured as a kind of second revelation alongside the Gospel of Christ or even as its continuation and contemporary form. Is there really an "eternal Germany" which is equal to God and which is the valid expression of His will for us today? Is the voice of the Aryan blood, i.e. the command of Adolf Hitler, equal to the commandment of God, or contained in it? Should the Church too be ruled authoritatively and militarily by "bishops", like little "Führers"? Is it really the province of the state to make a "total" claim on the life of men, and the Church's business only the right and duty to repeat and glorify this claim as divine and to reconcile and entrust men to it?

Whoever is surprised at these questions may well consider how little the evangelical Church in the last centuries has understood how to stand on her own feet, to repel alien spirits of the age, to set her light on a lamp-standard instead of under some bushel or other. So there was no cause for amazement at the fact that under the powerful impression of the new situation of 1933 a trend immediately appeared and was at first victorious in the evangelical Church (it called itself "German-Christian"). It thought it was able not only to be confident in the face of all these questions, but also to affirm them with the greatest enthusiasm. Christ *and* Hitler; the Bible *and* the glorious present! Cross *and* Swastika! The "S.A. (Storm Troopers) of Jesus Christ" thought they would win under this banner and had indeed some success at first. One of its people, the otherwise unknown and unimportant naval chaplain Ludwig Müller, set himself at the head of the evangelical Church as "State-bishop". The superior ecclesiastical powers in most regional Churches ended up after some fuss in the hands of this party. Its spirit, its words and slogans, its enthusiastic "and" ruled for a while up and down the country even in places where they seemed to have less to say or had even been rejected. Their purposes seemed to countless good and earnest Christians of all previous persuasions to be good. At that time there was good reason to be amazed at what an easily managed waxlike concern even the so-called "faithful" Christianity had obviously long since become, to allow itself to be treated in such a way.

But now there appeared on the heels of the "German-Christians" (still Christian in name) an unmistakable continuation of the earlier free thinkers and monists. This was a series of other religous groups (collected today in the "German Faith Movement") who thought they could affirm those questions better with quite open omission of Christ, Bible and Cross, and therefore set their heart on the founding of a "German National Church" with a non-Christian, even, as they deliberately said, a "pagan" content. According to § 24 of its party programme National Socialism and the German state which it rules today stands "on the ground of positive Christianity." But scholars are still arguing about the exact interpretation of this. What is certain is that both the "German-Christians" and these German pagans may be glad to have the far-reaching direct and indirect support of the organs of the National Socialist party and government. It is also certain that both these trends (and the German pagans even more than the "German-Christians"!) have on their side the course of National Socialism and thus of the whole historical development. Of course, the "Führer" has not yet expressed his personal decision.

The realization of what this putting into gear meant for the evangelical Church and the realization that the Church would have to resist it, dawned only very slowly and gradually. To begin with, it was only the revolutionary tempo and the somewhat lusty proceedings, especially of the "German-Christians," that gave offence in different circles. People were grieved at the failure of the attempt to make Pastor von Bodelschwingh State-bishop and thereby to ensure a peaceful continuance in Church life in mild harmony with the new age and order. People thought they should and could avoid basic decisions for a good while. They emphasized warmly and strongly that the Bible and the old Confessions of the Church must remain "untouched" even in the Church of the new Germany. But State-bishop Müller and the German-Christians were saying precisely this themselves. How far did people intend and desire anything different? At first they were not pointed either by the Bible or the old Confessions to the obligation to give clearly and decisively any other answer to the questions put so burningly, than that of the German-Christians. Here and there conflicts broke out over this or that. But it was the fight of a disbanded army with no united aim and no common way. There was room for suspicion that the opponents of reform in the Church as the National Socialists envisaged it were merely slow in comprehending the new age. And the opponents quite possibly hoped that these nonconformists would sooner or later abandon their scruples, which after all did not represent a fundamental intention.

But something else happened. How it came about is in the last resort hardly explicable. The senseless external pressure with which the new Church governments and the German Christians sought to establish themselves everywhere, the spiritual and intellectual inadequacy of all their leading people, surprise at the heathen backgrounds in this affair and perhaps too the beginnings of political disillusionment, even disappointment—all these things have, humanly speaking, certainly contributed. But there must have been some other factor at work when, at the beginning of 1934, the view was suddenly expressed that "Confession" in the evangelical Church must have some meaning beyond the devout repetition of what the godly fathers of the faith had expressed centuries ago in their times of need; that it must far rather mean an answer to contemporary questions which the Church today must utter with the certainty and compulsion of faith. It was not the old leaders of the Church, nor the theological faculties, it was neither the circles of the free Christian charitable and missionary organizations and societies nor the religious brotherhoods (nor was it the German "religious socialists"!) but it was very quietly, now here, now there, a few hundred pastors with their congregations, who formed free synods and parish conferences with the aim of giving an account to themselves and the rest of the Church, to the German-Christians and pagans, and to the National Socialist state itself, of what the Church today is and is not, what it wants and does not want. Quite spontaneously it became apparent under the pressure of the attack that there is something in the evangelical Church of whose existence in Germany and elsewhere we might with good cause have been doubtful, and not only in the past few years: namely, an independent knowledge, power and liveliness not subject to any worldly power, but rather, when necessary, defiant. It became apparent that the evangelical Church has a mission and a message which she may dishonour a thousand times but which she cannot ultimately abandon, which in an emergency forces itself on to the lips of Christians almost against their will and becomes a witness in positive statements with a clear Yes and No. It became apparent that there are situations in which even a weak, degenerate Church *must* confess and then indeed *can* confess.

Here are some of the statements which were heard at this time as the witness of the Confessing Church in Germany:

"We must turn our backs on the error that man can place his own honour beside or above the honour of God."

"We are not free to call anything 'God' which we think divine, but we must keep to God's revelation in Jesus Christ, as He is witnessed to us in Holy Scripture."

"We can offer unreserved trust to no good alongside God."

"We can only serve men by serving God."

"All of us live by God's grace and not by any human perfections".

"The message and order of the Church cannot therefore be directed according to any human aims, not even by the aim of a totalitarian State".

"The responsibility for her teaching, form and organization is in the hands of the congregation alone."

If these statements seem all too simple and obvious to anyone, let him remember that they have all been uttered here as answers to definite questions, in contradiction to definite errors, with an eye to basic decisions. In a time and situation when the very opposite is proclaimed in all the streets and in all the newspapers with an unprecedented display of power! No, the insight and the decision necessary for the public expression of such statements were simply and understandably lacking at this time and in this situation. And because those who did speak out were ultimately neither cleverer nor braver than other people, we may and must say that Christian faith performed a miracle in the confession which was suddenly heard here despite the repeated stupidity and weakness of its confessors.

For this also must finally be said: The story of the Confessing Church in the National Socialist Germany of these years is no glorious chronicle for its participants, no heroic or saintly story. What became evident was just a thin red thread of evangelical clarity, loyalty and courage. It has become stronger with time but also even thinner. And it has been and is always being buried by whole avalanches of most remarkable unclarity, by subtle political foresight and irresolution, by misplaced "love", by futile activity and equally futile clumsiness. The time-honoured connection of the Gospel with human reason, of the Church with the State, has shown itself in all its danger in the Confessing Church too. We can and must reproach this Confessing Church for not recognizing the enemy early on in its real dangerousness and for not unambiguously and forcefully opposing to him early on the Word of God, which judges human deceit and injustice, as was her duty as the Church of Jesus Christ. She has fought hard to a certain extent for the freedom and purity of her proclamation, but she has, for instance, remained silent on the action against the Jews, on the amazing treatment of political opponents, on the suppression of the freedom of the press in the new Germany and on so much else against which the Old Testament prophets would certainly have spoken out. Her path in its own particular course has been, when examined closely, almost a continuous series of errors, confusions, and disappointments. We can and must therefore call her "Confession" very unsatisfying. How will her struggle end? Remembering the human factor, it is not only very possible but very probable that it will end with a lazy compromise.

In the final instance we can perhaps only be amazed and glad that the inward and outward weakness of Christianity did not prove even greater at this time. But it seems to me that we shall have reason to be thankful not only because of that red thread, but also because this bit of Church history has brought one fact into the open so clearly: In the Church, glory belongs to God alone. In the midst of all human infidelity, God has proved faithful here once again. No-one who followed this struggle with attention, participation and comprehension will be able to forget that. And has the Church not always lived, does she not live in all places, by the hope which, despairing of herself, she sets in the Lord alone?

V

THE GERMAN CONFESSING CHURCH 1935-36.[1]

AFTER BEGINNING IN the *Zwingli-Kalender* of 1936 to tell readers about the Confessing Church in National Socialist Germany, I am glad to be able to continue my report. I write with more joy than last year because, along with all the anxiety with which one must still think of the events out there and in a certain respect even more than before, on the decisive point there is better news.

Many people in Switzerland will have noticed that the reports in our political newspapers on Church events in Germany have, apart from a few exceptional occasions, become much less frequent in the past year than before and have sometimes disappeared almost entirely for long periods. Nothing would be further from the truth than to draw the conclusion from this that the struggle is over or coming to an end.

One reason for the phenomenon is quite simply that the police restriction, or even suppression, of the press and also hindrance of the Confessing Church's half-public reporting organization has become considerably stricter in the past year and also that the reports which happen to come the way of the foreign correspondents of our papers through other channels can only be general and colourless. What people said two or three years ago more in jest than in earnest has already got a little truth in it: The Confessing Church now exists actually in the "Catacombs" so far as its most important organs and activities are concerned; i.e. away from the public spheres known and accessible to everybody.

The other and more important reason is that the questions which have occupied the Confessing Church during the past year have become increasingly material, i.e. seriously ecclesiastical questions, which lacked interest because of the lack of expert knowledge on the part of most correspondents and editors of our newspapers, and not least the majority of our newspaper readers, in evaluating and judging these questions. I regard this as a sign of progress. No-one, who knew what was and still is at stake, could be more than partly glad at the "interest" which our

[1] *Zwingli-Kalender.* 1937, pp. 67-69. Written summer, 1936.

press took for some time in the "German Church struggle". It is only to be expected that the affair should in time become boring for those who think they can understand and discuss Church matters from outside the Church and questions of faith from outside faith. This "Church conflict" has become more secret, precisely because it has become more basic.

When I wrote about it a year ago, I did not conceal how much basic unclarity continued to burden the Confessing Church despite all its good intentions; and I can now admit that my thoughts on the subject were far more painful than I liked to say in public. We did not even know for sure whether we were wanting to make our own confession to the Gospel and leave everything else to the Gospel itself or to save the Church by means of supposedly clever adaptations and concessions. In this uncertainty the Confessing Church found itself, one unhappy November day in 1934, given an administration at whose head was the Bishop of Hanover, Marahrens. Its activity, which lasted over a year, was more like that of a liquidation commission than of an executive board. More than one of its announcements was practically indistinguishable from those of the German-Christians. In this uncertainty the two Reformed Churches of East Frisia and Lippe were unfortunately manœuvring (and are still doing so, to this day) against the old Heidelberg catechism, despite all assurances of loyalty. The National Synod held in Augsburg in June 1935[1] still stood under the cloud of this uncertainty.

Now it is not that this obscurity has since then simply disappeared. But the clarity and obscurity have defined themselves over against each other quite differently from what was the case a year ago. This obscurity as such, remarkable as it may sound, has assumed a definite, sharply outlined shape, and now there is a definite line against it, an energetic opposition. Much chaff (perhaps not yet all) has been separated from the corn. Everywhere the ranks of the Confessing Church have become narrower, but also everywhere more concentrated. It is now known in these ranks what is expected and not expected of the witness to Jesus Christ in National Socialist Germany. That is the decidedly better news I have to report today. And this is how it came about:

In the autumn of 1935 the Hitler Government suddenly considered it right to strike a new course in its suppression of the Evangelical Church. A special Church Ministry was set up under the leadership of

[1] The third Confessional Synod of the German Evangelical Church, June 4–6

48

the former Law officer Kerrl, with the commission to provide a middle way between the two "groups," the hitherto favoured German-Christians and the Confessing Church, and thus to make peace in the Church. With an almost audible explosion Reichsbishop Müller, once appointed so powerfully, was admittedly not dismissed, but (he had long since become an impossible figure) placed in a position of harmless retirement, and the "assistant bishops" in the various districts fared similarly. One of them gave as the explanation of his retirement, that he intended to devote himself henceforth to collecting beetles. Everywhere they were replaced by so-called "Church-committees,"composed by the new Church Minister more or less equally of representatives of the two "groups" as well as of all kinds of former neutrals.

At the head of the State's Church-committee there was appointed, or had himself appointed, the 76-year-old General Superintendent Zoellner, who had been in retirement for six years—a powerful fighter during three decades for what was at that time called "positive" theology. The event was doubtless a first clear success for the resistance of the Confessing Church. The State—this State!—gave way. Despite all the weakness and insecurity, the Confessing Church did not fight and suffer in vain when they were determined not to be satisfied with their success but to fight and suffer all the more. Or on the other hand, could, should,—must they, tired of the long dispute, retire to winter quarters? This was the question that led to the distinction between obscurity and clarity.

There were all those who still called the programme of the German-Christians—Christ and Hitler—basically good, and who only took offence at the robust methods and personalities of the German-Christians, especially those of the "Reibi".[1] There were those who had understood the confessional declarations at Barmen and Dahlem about the sole validity of Holy Scripture and about the Church's freedom to govern itself, merely as the powerful words of a fine resolution which, however, could be shelved again on occasion, and who had always understood the whole Confessing Church itself only as a "group" alongside which there might well be other "groups" without confession or with other confessions. There were those who still set their hopes on the supposedly "positive Christianity" of the National Socialist State, despite its long-established theoretical and practical paganism, or those who were still afraid of the threat which also obviously stood behind

---

[1] *i.e.* Rei[chs]bi[schof]—State-bishop.

Kerrl's programme. There were those who, as supposed Lutherans, had long been anxiously awaiting the moment which would bring them to an understanding with the authorities who, for them, were ordained of God. Or finally, there were those who did not credit their congregations or even themselves with the strength for further endurance. All these now fell into line, some hesitatingly, others with jaunty step, with Bishop Marahrens at their head, and became members of Church-committees or were ready to work in co-operation with them.

One cannot be thankful enough for the erection of this sign which divided the spirits—that is, in view of what was happening on the other side. The Confessing Church as a whole submitted to the committees as little as it had previously done to the Reichsbishop, and used the argument that they were debarred by the confession from letting themselves be governed by the State (even as mediated by such "positive" theologians!) and be treated, not as the lawful evangelical Church, but as a "group" in a partly evangelical, partly German-Christian, Church. Certainly, not a single one of the men responsible was happy about the dispute ("pastors' quarrels"!), but it was a matter of standing quite soberly to the testimony which had been taken before the world in 1934. The Confessing Church had declared at the State Synod at Oeynhausen, held in February 1936, that it was not in a position to do anything different in regard to the new system. The Church government of Marahrens retreated. In its place came men who will go seriously and resolutely along the right path, and who have already begun to do so.

It cannot be very easy for the Swiss to understand these events. Yet the opinions and the system of obscurity from which the Confessing Church has once more turned aside are pretty much the opinions and system of our Swiss established Church. What else do we see than that the Church now consists of "groups" and that it can therefore neither venture nor have a confession? What else do we see than that one may give honour in the Church just as much to Christ alone as to Christ and other Lords. The one difference is that we have no Kerrl to force the matter on us, but hitherto we have wanted to have it so ourselves. Many of us may easily feel the behaviour of the German Confessing Church somewhat unruly and abrupt, whereas previously we were not unsympathetic. Yet we should not fail to reflect on what the Church properly is, and whether a Church can exist and behave any differently from what the German Confessing Church has done this year.

I should very much like to know what the continuation of this

Church history, on which I may perhaps be reporting next year, will look like. Today, in fact, one cannot foresee it. One cannot imagine easily and precisely the magnitude of the inward and outward difficulties in which the Confessing Church still really finds itself. It may be that many more, even of those who in these years have been brave in their opposition to this gross power, will weaken when confronted with the acute temptation of the committee's programme and will collapse. It may be that the National Socialist State is only waiting for the end of the Olympic Games (i.e. for the departure of the many foreigners now staying in Germany) before letting fly against the Confessing Church, as it has done against other "intractables". It may be that the centuries-old opposition between Lutherans and Reformed in the Confessing Church is causing many unnecessary hindrances. It may be that the whole thing will yet end with a worthless compromise. A year ago, under the pressure of certain observations in the *Zwingli-Kalender*, I designated the latter as "very probable". But today I could only call it possible.

In the sifting of this year it has been shown that there is no lack of a slight but strong band of pastors and congregations, who are prepared for new loyalty and new action. Nor is there lacking a new and promising generation of theologians, nor of wise and energetic leaders. It has been shown that the decisions of 1934 (Barmen and Dahlem)[1] have an inner weight and binding power. It has been shown that there is an ever-growing consciousness that the Church cannot serve two masters and that she proceeds most securely when she draws all the conclusions offered to her out of this situation vis-à-vis a state which wants things completely different. It has been shown that even the genuine Lutherans and the genuine Reformed (to which those who call themselves so most enthusiastically do not belong) can help one another instead of laying stumbling-blocks in each other's paths. Most of all it has been shown in this year that the Word of God wonderfully sustains those who are ready to be sustained by it.

When one keeps all this before one's eyes, one may well reckon with the possibility of a humanly speaking unfavourable outcome of the matter, for on this earth no certainty is completely certain. But yet

---

[1] Synods of Barmen (May 29-31) and Dahlem (October 19-20). For very full accounts and the documents see Gerhard Niemöller: *Die erste Bekenntnissynode der Deutschen Evangelischen Kirche zu Barmen* (AGK 6-7, 1959), and Wilhelm Niemöller: *Die zweite Bekenntnissynode der Deutschen Evangelischen Kirche zu Dahlem* (AGK 3, 1958).

one will be calm at the thought of this possibility: Here there has been, and there is being, cast forth a seed which will one day bear fruit. When and how? *Dominus providebit.* May the Swiss contemporaries then not live as those who celebrate Calvin and the battles of the far-away sixteenth century, only to turn aside their eyes from the need and hope of a Church in the present!

VI

THE WAR AGAINST THE
EVANGELICAL CHURCH IN GERMANY[1]

THIS IS A good time and opportunity to say a further word about this matter which, hidden for most of us behind the mists of unskilful and even misleading reporting, is taking its consistent course. I shall do so in the form of a short commentary on the latest communications that have come through the press.

Since about the autumn of the previous year, the State Party and Secret Police of the Third Reich have embarked upon a new attack, obviously centrally inspired and directed, on the Evangelical Church. It must not be overlooked that this attack affects in the first place the so-called Confessing Church (by which is meant many different degrees of those determined to resist), which must in the first place endure and defend itself, however thorough the attack may be. And that in such a way that sooner or later it will be difficult to deny that the affair cannot be basically distinguished from a war against the Church and its substance, such as is being waged with other methods in Russia. Difficult to deny, I mean, not only by the Zoellner Church Committees set up by the State itself, not only by the ever-optimistic Lutheran Bishops of Bavaria, Württemberg, etc., along with the "intact" Churches of their provinces, but also by the faithful and the upright among the broad mass of the uncommitted of all kinds, as well as in the ranks of the law-abiding "German-Christians", even from their previous standpoint of no or hardly any confession.

The German, or National Socialist, method, which has become more and more fluid in the last months, is as follows:

1. First of all, they (by which is meant the inextricable mixture of State, Party and Secret Police which in Germany is in possession of public power) keep the semblance of maintaining official toleration, even acknowledgement, even solicitude, of the organization of the Church as such. Does this not mean in the programme of the N.S.D.A.P.,[2]

---

[1] Published in the Zürich newspaper *Neue Zürcher Zeitung*, Feb. 2, 1937.

[2] *Nationalsozialistische deutsche Arbeiter-partei* (*i.e.* the National Socialist Party).

afterwards as well as before, winning the confidence of all the innocent, and getting them to believe that the party is taking its stand on the platform of "positive Christianity"? In crises—say if foreign opinion makes itself noticeably unpleasant—they will be in a position to return to this semblance, and from a distance will easily create the impression, even among innumerable people in Germany itself (among all those at least who desire peace at any price in this sphere and among all friends of order) that everything necessary and reasonable, or at least nothing openly bad, is happening. It was on these lines, and for the preservation of this appearance, that Kerrl's Ministry for Church Affairs and the Zoellner Committee were set up thirteen months ago: "for the pacification" of the Church, as they called it then.

The outcome is that today, where these committees (such exceptions were due to the worthy people who, like Zoellner himself, were short-sighted enough to give their name to this matter) wanted, and strove for, something serious, the Church-minister each time intervened to prevent it. However, they, and through them the public power, succeeded in introducing some at least temporary and partial confusion into the ranks of the Confessing Church—in breathing new life into the spirits of indolence and opportunism, and most of all in giving to the whole National Socialist Church policy, at home and abroad, an exceedingly respectable, not to say venerable, aspect by which so many Swiss people were beautifully taken in. They relied on the fact that this, and not "pacification", was from the beginning the object of the exercise, and that, if it should ever be worn out, there would certainly not be any difficulty in replacing it by something similar.

2. All flagrant acts of force are eschewed as far as possible. No-one is shot. Relatively few are removed, banished or even imprisoned. The reader of foreign newspapers must wait in vain for Russian or Spanish news of terror and can therefore slumber on. What they actually do is this: the last legitimate freedoms of the press and of meeting together left to the Confessing Church are removed. But they also limit the possibilities for movement, communication and expression of the remaining Church courts and groups (including even those of the State Church committee set up by the State itself) lest they should show some signs of Church responsibility. Even Marahrens in Bremen and Meiser in Erfurt are forbidden to speak. And then (after the parts had been made as unequal as possible by means of the magic word of the Secret Police, "In defence of the State and People") there was started (under the Reich Ministry of Propaganda) a really intense bombardment of literary and

rhetorical insinuations, accusations and insults—precisely against what constitutes the life of the Church, even if she has fallen into heresy and superstition, far less if she is a conscientious, resolute and confessing Church.

I am reluctant to provide examples of this literature ("Lightning," "Breakthrough", "Storm Centre"—these pamphlets all had such names) or of the speeches of Ley, Streicher, Sauchel, etc. The thought running through them is always the same: Christianity equals Judaism; Judaism equals Bolshevism; Bolshevism equals enmity against the people. Therefore away with Christianity! As there is no fear of a well-grounded protest from the other side, these writers and speakers can treat things delightfully simply.

But one has to remember: the numbers of the readers of each of these pamphlets run into hundreds of thousands. The speakers engaged in this business are not the first and best, but the high and highest State and Party officials. And when in the Third Reich a subject is spoken about so unanimously and under such uniform police toleration, this is not accidental, but quite deliberate. Can the intention here be any other than that, not perhaps of convincing, but of accustoming the German public (according to the well-known recipe!) by continual impolite dirges, to the fact that the rather undifferentiated "Christianity" under attack is a dangerous and damnable thing?

Of course, it cannot be that the real life of the Church could be damaged or even affected by all this. But what will be the effect of it on countless unthinking people who are not alive to this journalistic and rhetorical treatment? We can even regard it as very good for the Church itself to have to keep silent during it all—it has often spoken too much. But this is no excuse for the aggressors.

It is a fact that the present German State through its press is oppressing the Church quite ruthlessly and at the same time is forbidding her to speak against this oppression. It is a fact that Streicher can talk[1] and even Zoellner (not to mention the Confessing Church) must keep quiet in public. It is a fact that the most harmless Sunday papers are made to conform and have even been suppressed if they dared to call a spade anything like a spade. It is a fact that even counter-declarations in the course of a service, and thus literally within the church walls, can only take place with the danger of police interference and punishment. It is a fact that the most blatant blasphemy in present-day Germany is

---

[1] *i.e.* as editor of the defamatory and pornographic Nazi paper, *Der Stürmer*.

unrestrained, and that the Church is prevented from speaking against it.

This is what happens behind the scenes of the relationship, apparently so harmlessly ordered, between Church and State.

3. Externally independent of this "spiritual" conflict, there is in the sphere of cultural and educational policy a whole system of direct and indirect measures in motion which bit by bit (one would think one was back in the time of the *Kulturkampf*[1], save that the procedure has become much more energetic) is pursuing the plain object of isolating the Church so thoroughly and making it so superfluous that sooner or later the justification for its formal removal will seem evident.

The direction of National Socialist Church policy, at any rate towards the Evangelical Church, has changed from what was proclaimed in 1933 by the "German-Christians". At that time they wanted to "capture" the Church. Today we must make no mistake that they still want only to destroy it in favour of a more or less sentimental reverence for the State, and in favour of the ethos of the "political soldier", in which the German man is to recognize his ultimate destiny, something which will have nothing more at all to do with the Church, and to whose establishment probably the "German-Christians", whether mild, middle or strict, the "German Faith Movement," along with all Rosenbergians[2] and with the enterprises of that wild married couple, the Ludendorffs[3], are destined to provide only a prelude.

Abroad it should not be expected that this destruction will be heard as a big bang. The matter has rightly been compared to the demolition and rebuilding of a railway bridge, over which the traveller will one day pass without noticing that it is no longer the old, but a new bridge.

In what follows I am describing quite literally how that is being done: First the Church has, by a continual cutting of the cords which have so far bound her to the life of the nation, to be banished into an allegedly freely bestowed inner room of private devotion and ceremony. Then the resulting vacuum has to be filled up with all kinds of eccentric substitutes. The next step is to point out emphatically the meaninglessness of these private concerns. Then the officials and party members have to have it sufficiently impressed upon them that this private concern could hardly be their business, and that neutrality towards it

[1] The conflict between the German State under Bismarck and the Roman Catholic Church.

[2] Followers of Rosenberg's "Blood and Folk" ideology.

[3] General Ludendorff and his wife created an anti-Christian and pagan mysticism, the *Tannenberg-bund*.

would be a good thing, withdrawal from the Church perhaps the best thing. Every voice which wants to draw attention to what is going on has to be rendered suspect of scandalous trouble-making and silenced.

The indisputable power and might to do all this are certainly at their disposal. The Church then will one day have become an association of a few unwordly eccentrics and old people. No-one will need to go to the lengths of exterminating them, like the wicked Bolshevists, because their company will go into a decline and disintegrate of its own accord within a generation. And to push the matter further, one needs only now and then to narrow down the inner-room of the Church more and more, and to tighten more and more the definition of what this permitted devotion and ceremony can be.

It is clear that the machinery for this last function does not always work quite noiselessly, and that on such occasions the significance of the whole process can become dimly noticeable for a moment. Where was respect merely for the proper and inner affairs of the Church, when they wanted at that time to demand of her, and of the Kerrl and Zoellner system imposed on her, quite simply capitulation to the "German-Christians"? What is the good of the freedom of doctrine theoretically allowed to the Church, when actually not only every opposition raised in the name of this teaching against the State's religious policy (or even against earlier measures!), but gradually also the plain and positive assertion of Biblical truths such as the universality of baptism, the seriousness of sin, the validity of the Old Testament and the commandment to humility, etc., are rejected with horror as a politically detestable undertaking, repugnant to the moral sensibility of our people, and for which the Church is summoned "to beat her breast in confession"?—confessing, that is, that it will be her own fault if she one day ceases to be the Church of the German people through adhering to such teaching.

Is it not an interference in a sphere which should be considered the specific sphere of the Church, when the teaching of religion in State schools is changed more and more into a lesson on the fight against the "Jewish-Asiatic world picture" of Christianity? Or when on November 17, the Reich Minister of Culture orders with one stroke of the pen that, in future, theological students shall be forbidden, on pain of permanent expulsion from the State university, to take part in any of the organized instruction arranged by the Confessing Church? Or when recently even conferences for the theological instruction of pastors and other Church members were methodically forbidden and suppressed? Or when, on the morning of December 14, the secret police of Elberfeld, unannounced, without the authorization of a written order and without any higher power giving its reasons, disturbs the theological school of that town in the middle of its lectures and then seals up its doors as a sign that it is "closed" and "dissolved" and that its teachers and pupils are dispersed? (a course such tyrants have always loved to take).

What did these things mean? They meant very palpably that the intended development was obviously still not going fast enough for them and should therefore be accelerated. It had not proved effective enough to expel nearly all the elements true to the confession from the State theological faculties, especially in Prussia, and to give their places to blind young people who, for the sake of professorships, were only too willing to lecture on the German-Christian heresy. Yet the Church had become even stronger than had been thought. She had not capitulated. Nor was she content to entrust her theological youth to, say, the eternally neutral wisdom of the faculties at Tübingen and Erlangen, till now still tolerably "intact". From her own strength and with her own means she had made opportunities of proclaiming and hearing the real, unadulterated and unabridged Christian teaching, and the big crowd which these emergency institutions drew, and the effect which they had, were an open secret. So they had now to encroach a bit deeper into the ostensibly respected inner room of the Church, so as to destroy these institutions also. The fact that real Christian teaching was renewing and maintaining itself in such a way from within itself did not harmonize with the intended demolition programme, and could therefore also not be a part of the private devotion and ceremony which were provisionally still permitted. . . !

Such things as these are experienced also in evangelical Churches abroad. But evangelical Churches abroad are in general—and this must be said—remarkably apathetic towards the need of their sister Church in Germany. A well-known Swiss pastor, who was staying at the end of the year in one of the centres of the German Church struggle, was asked there if the oppressed Evangelical Church in Germany was being prayed for at services in Switzerland. He had to reply truthfully that this was not happening so far as he knew. I myself have seen how at the Calvin Jubilee in Geneva last summer, the presence and address of a representative of the German Confessing Church had to some extent to be smuggled in against the wishes of the inner circle, who were tuned in to peaceful festivity, and how this was obviously taken by them as a disturbing of the—Calvin Jubilee!

And to this day the ecumenical Church committees in this same Geneva still do not seem to have come clean on whether the question of the German Confessing Church actually concerns them, or whether it is not, as the question merely of a certain theology, at once so discredited that it would be most advisable to keep a safe middle path between it and Zoellner till it becomes clear which side has the "stronger battalions". While I am of the opinion that this official apathy (and diplomacy!) will avenge itself one day, I will not hide the fact that I have found decidedly more heart and understanding for the affair in a whole number of Swiss parishes.

Finally, moreover, we may repeat with the same certainty what we said frequently on the occasion of the setting up of Kerrl's Church Ministry: The Confessing Church will continue to exist. And that with or without the support of evangelicals abroad! What I said about this was said for their sakes and not Germany's. The Confessing Church, and in and with it the German Evangelical Church as such, will continue to exist. All that was said at that time in proof of this statement and that since then has proved true clearly enough, is true today. As long and as far as a Church is a confessing Church, it will be destroyed neither by cunning nor by force, neither with powerful propaganda nor with police truncheons.

We must wish this Church just one thing: that it should be, and should become much more intensively, in fact and in truth, what she is—the Confessing Church. As such the German Evangelical Church declared at the Synod of Breslau[1], as we now know, that, with God's help, everything should and would continue: the preaching of the Gospel, alongside which there is nothing else, and also assembly and instruction in the parishes and therefore also the renewal of Christian doctrine from out of itself and its eternal sources, and therefore also theological schools and instruction weeks! Just as those who declared this have hitherto made themselves well-known, we may safely suppose that they will be men enough to act in accordance with their words.

At the same time, no thoughtful onlooker will fail to recognize that the whole attack by the other side, which today has become so energetic

---

[1] The fourth Confessional Synod of the Evangelical Church of the Old Prussian Union, December 16–18, 1936. See G. Niemöller, *Die Synode zu Halle 1937* (AGK 11, 1963), p. 29.

and ingenious, is bearing witness more, very much more, to its nervousness, which for various reasons is on the increase, than to a clean conscience and the natural confidence of a representative of a good case.

VII

THE GERMAN CONFESSING CHURCH 1936–37.[1]

In LOOKING BACK over this last year, it may be said without false optimism that the events on the Church battlefield of our northern neighbour have developed for the better. The external oppression under which the Church is standing has admittedly become stronger, the pagan propaganda ("Schwarze Korps", Ludendorff etc.) still more intensive, the attitude of the radical wing of the "German-Christians" (Thüringian Leadership, Professor Hirsch in Göttingen etc.) still more radical, the police interference and attacks still more frequent and startling (the closing of the theological schools in Elberfeld and Berlin, the ban on the "evangelical weeks" etc.), the distress in the parishes and vicarages still greater as a result—and for that reason still greater also the drain on nervous energy, by now serious, with its associated dangers of fatigue on the one hand and of over-excitement on the other.

But behind and despite this exterior side, which is all that is visible to foreign countries, a series of events has happened or opened up, which point to the fact that it is a good thing to be thrown back in this way more and more on the Word of God alone, as has happened and is happening in these years to our evangelical (and with them perhaps also our catholic) fellow-Christians in present-day Germany.

It was reported in last year's *Zwingli-Kalender* how the Confessing Church in the autumn of 1935 was led into temptation by the setting up of neutral "Church committees", through which it was to be brought as a "group" under one roof with the "German-Christians", who denied the evangelical faith, and through whose mediation the State thought it could once more lay its hand on the internal affairs of the Church. But it could be reported at the same time how the Confessing Church set itself in a position of defence against this undertaking at the Reich Synod of Oeynhausen.

The new "Provisional Leadership of the German Evangelical Church" set up at that time (and remarkably efficient in its work) had to battle against the most difficult external and in particular internal hindrances,

[1] *Zwingli-Kalender*, 1938, pp. 36–39. Written summer 1937.

in order to procure merely respect and execution for the decisions of Oeynhausen. In particular the miserable "parish-pump policy" of the Lutherans outside the Prussian Union Church proved to be a ponderous brake. The attempts at compromise and the "back-handers" which, from this side, checked the inevitable course of things, can remain unmentioned here. Nevertheless, the Church committees have in fact won no authority for themselves. Their peak was reached when on February 12, 1937, one year after the Oeynhausen Synod, the state's Church Committee under the leadership of Dr. Zoellner had to resign its commission into the hands of Church-Minister Kerrl.

The whole system of Church committees was shaken to its foundations, and, after some to-ing and fro-ing, the remnants of this half and half solution (once so dangerous or, from another point of view, so full of promise) disappeared from the scene in the second half of June. This attack may have been repelled.

The new leadership of the Confessing Church, however, had already shown in the summer of 1936 that it was not willing to carry on the passive restraint of its predecessors towards the State's isolation of the Church, and also towards the general condition of German affairs. That is to say, it turned to Adolf Hitler himself with a direct petition in which it openly expressed (for the first time without any "Yes-but") not only the Church's protest in regard to all the interference with her existence and activity, but also, arising out of that, (in this way likewise for the first time) the Christian accusation against the general injury to law and humanity which in the Third Reich had become systematic.

Countless people, even in Germany itself, had long been waiting for such a word. It came late, but it came. However much one may, perhaps from the safety of Switzerland, have wished for an even stronger tone, we shall no longer in future be able to accuse the Confessing Church of being silent in this matter.

The result showed the complete darkness of the situation. It is not known whether this petition reached the "Führer", even in a literal sense. And, above all, it is not known how it got spread abroad in Europe. At any rate the manager in the office of the "Provisional Church leadership", Dr. Weissler, the former Director of Provincial Courts, had to pay for this with his life. He was arrested on the accusation of having occasioned this publication. No proof was produced, nor did he have any trial. He was murdered at the concentration camp of Oranienburg on February 19, 1937, and as usual the cause of death was given as "suicide". Weissler was a baptized Jew. It is a painful but true fact that the leadership of the Lutheran regional Church had no worse worry in this matter than how to remove itself as far as possible from the Berlin leadership of the Confessing Church, which had been "compromised" in this way.

A further step for the better in another direction was shown by the decisions of the Prussian Synod held at the beginning of May 1937 in Halle. Externally these formed the continuation of the Synod of Breslau held shortly before Christmas 1936, at which the Church decided that, in view of the impossible position in the German theological faculties, it would in future take into its own hands the training of the rising theological generation. In Halle they were occupied with an old worry of the Prussian Church, but one which had become burning in the stormy present, that is, the question of the confessions united in it rather hastily and superficially in 1817: in other words, the union of the "Lutherans" and "Reformed", alongside whom a "united" Church had in time acquired the character of a sort of third Confession: an instructive example of how mistakenly effected peace treaties will only increase the conflict. What can these separations signify, what can they not signify today? The present Church conflict is a necessity, so that clear understanding and a clear confession may for the first time be set over against the disorder and uncertainty which prevails in this sphere.

The Synod of Halle arose out of the fact that members of the Prussian Lutheran, Reformed and "United" Churches had actually in the past year believed and confessed, suffered and struggled as one Church. It confirmed this fact: that there should no longer be any talk of two Churches in Prussia divided between Lutherans and Reformed; in particular full Inter-communion between the two or the three parts (despite the different doctrines of Holy Communion) should henceforth be lawful and necessary. Despite differing doctrines! That is to say, the different old Confessions are not perhaps losing their power where hitherto they have been valid: on the contrary the parishes are invited to decide, as far as possible, for one or other of the "confessional positions" (in practice, for Luther's or for the Heidelberg Catechism) and therefore to stand in one way or another in a definite relationship with the Reformation and under a definite ordering of the doctrine valid in its confessions. The partial contradiction of these doctrines must no longer be understood as a Church-splitting conflict, though there will have to be further work under the presupposition of the

63

common faith and therefore in peace, with the aim of removing the contradiction.

The decisions of this Synod (unfortunately not at first stretching over the whole of Germany, but only in Prussia) may well find a particularly sympathetic welcome from us in Switzerland. We are thinking that, like the Prussians from 1817 to 1937, we too live in a Church in which contradictions are possible and real, and which make her character as a Church more than doubtful. A practical application of this might be obvious. Might a path like that trodden in Halle not be commanded us also? In fact the decisions of Halle are in their way just as important and meaningful as the common confession of faith against the errors of the time that was discovered and expressed three years ago in Barmen. We must not disregard the order in which this happened. The common confession of faith had to come first; then, and consequently, the union in freedom and the freedom in union. There will certainly be no other way to peace in the Church for us in Switzerland either.

One aspect of German Church history in the year 1936–37 which should also not be forgotten is that at this time the Evangelical Church was more than once forced to become clearly aware, whether she would or no, that she lived next door to the Roman Catholic Church, which was in different, though in effect similar, straits. Even evangelical Christians can scarcely be in doubt that the "monastery trials"[1], with which the National Socialist system sought to attack the Catholic Church, are an injustice which reminds one only too well of the "Stop thief!" of the Reichstag Fire Trial of 1933. But here we are treading on dangerous grounds. One can, of course, ask whether Catholicism might not have been able to come to terms with and even befriend certain basic ideas of a National Socialist Christianity, if only they had been put forward with somewhat more moderation and prudence— basic ideas with which the Evangelical Church would under no circumstances have had any dealings if its opponent had not driven things along so madly.

But however this may be, in fact Catholicism in Germany today is also attacked at its very heart, pressed into a defensive position and into a common front with the evangelical Confessing Church. This fact found remarkable expression in the Papal Encyclical[2] read from all

[1] The trials of members of religious houses on various charges of currency-smuggling and immorality.

[2] *Mit brennender Sorge*. The central and mainly relevant passages are given in Duncan-Jones, pp. 290–297.

Catholic pulpits on Palm Sunday 1937, in that, alongside all its deviations, it was remarkably reminiscent of the decisive convictions which the Confessing Church had been fighting for, all these years. Also the common ground of the Christian confession to Jesus Christ as the Son of God was expressly established by that very honourable and brave Bishop Graf Galen, in a public address in Münster in Westphalia. In this matter, we shall do well to "wait and see" as the Englishman says. For here too the facts must be allowed to speak for themselves.

When the Reich's Church Committee resigned, the Church Minister, Kerrl, was in fact already on the point of introducing a State Church dictatorship, which would then inevitably have resulted in a general persecution. In this case, as sometimes earlier, it has not emerged which events or relationships hindered or, far more, diverted the apparently inescapable development. In short, it came about that the "Führer" himself intervened at the last moment with the proclamation of new elections, which he promised would be free, for a future General Synod. No-one, really no-one, (and perhaps not even he himself!) knows how he really thought this up, in view of the Church decisions and splits which had just happened. Perhaps by the time this *Kalender* appears, we shall be wiser in this respect. Perhaps at least in a year's time. But not perhaps even then.

For the present, at any rate, things have become strangely quiet again since this announcement, which has never been given an authoritative interpretation. Once more we must bewail the fact that even in this dangerous situation the Lutheran regional Churches have tried as usual (unsuccessfully of course) to go their own way in a not very lovely way. One thing is certain. (The position of the Confessing Church has since strengthened so much both internally and externally that one can venture on a little prophecy—with the reservations which are, of course, necessary). The leaders and parishes of the Confessing Church will not find themselves ready to compromise on their basic and practical denial of "German-Christianity's" membership of the Evangelical Church, even in face of a "crushing majority" at this forthcoming "free" election. What will happen then, God knows. Yet we must reckon with the fact that this "free" election may never take place at all.

But, even if the darkness should become still greater, we cannot imagine that our evangelical brothers in Germany could be let down by Him in whom alone they must and may place their trust evermore.

VIII

THE GERMAN CONFESSING CHURCH 1937-38[1].

THE CONFESSING CHURCH in Germany has a hard year behind it. The darkness which was mentioned at the end of my last report has become appreciably greater. The internal and external participation of all who realize what the struggle is about should increase, not decrease.

In the spring of 1937, as was reported last year, Hitler arranged, with a great deal of pomp, "free" elections for the Church. All sorts of clever people, even among us, were foolish enough to see a wonderful proof of his desire for peace and justice in this announcement, unquestionably dangerous as things were. However that may be, there has been no further mention of these elections, despite Hitler's speech. The continual chopping and changing practised by the government in the means it uses to overcome in the conflict has also continued and has further revealed its inward uncertainty on the Church issue. The unheard-of physical power which it controls and the ruthlessness with which it uses this power has, through this vacillation in its employment, (and perhaps precisely in this way), had the effect of exciting, paralysing and tiring the Confessing Church.

In the summer and autumn of 1937 the picture of the struggle was governed by a haphazard yet impressive wave of police arrests and longer or shorter imprisonments, by which they tried, especially in Prussia, to intimidate the clergy and congregations of the Confessing Church. At times more than a third of the officiating clergy in East Prussia are said to have been behind lock and key. The hardest hit victim of this procedure was Martin Niemöller, the pastor in Dahlem, a former naval officer proved in the war and with unquestionable nationalistic sentiments, who has now, as preacher and leader in the Church struggle, stood his ground with particular courage and openness. Arrested at the end of June 1937 he had to wait till January 1938 for the trial promised him as rebel and traitor. He was let off by the judge with a light punishment, with the explanation that he had served his sentence while being held for enquiries. Immediately, he

---

[1] *Zwingli-Kalender*, 1939, pp. 61-63. Written summer 1938.

was arrested by the Gestapo, which is bound by no law and justice, and sent without charge or sentence to a concentration camp, from which so far none of the numerous petitions and deputations from Germany itself and still less the various private and public actions from abroad have been able to free him, abandoned as he is to the personal favour or disfavour of Hitler himself. We know that, in the concentration camp, as earlier in prison, he is richly comforted by the Word of God, despite the human hopelessness of his situation. But no-one (especially any naïve travellers in Germany) should forget for one moment that he is there and what his situation is: in our very midst a man who is plainly and simply suffering brutal injustice for the sake of our evangelical faith.

For the rest, the struggle was not at first waged on these lines. From November 1937 onwards the number of arrests began to drop. Instead, the efforts of the State were concentrated on the one hand on disturbance by the police, for instance the destruction of the little administrative machinery painfully created by the Confessing Church, of communication between the consistories, both among themselves and with the congregations, of all public co-operation by the many scattered groups and individuals who are as determined as ever to preserve the insights which they have won and maintained since 1933. In this respect the authorities have had less success than was to be expected. That they could have had a little success is obvious. The State has, on the other hand, made new attempts to strengthen the position of the still existing Church authorities (which are orientated around or influenced by the German-Christians) over against the Confessing Church by taking new administrative measures which have been especially oppressive from the economic point of view. By reason of these, for example, many hundreds of young clergymen, examined and ordained by the consistories, have been brought close to starvation, so that they have been forced to submit to the Church government which opposes the Confession and to the religious, cultural and political will of the National Socialist state. The Confessing Church is known still to exist in the sphere of the general Established Church. How efficiently the thumbscrew will be used, how great on the other hand the temptation to all sorts of major and minor concessions may be, can easily be imagined. And anyone inclined to be surprised at the occasionally occurring concessions should ask himself whether he too would be in a position to resist this thumbscrew in the circumstances.

When in the spring of 1938 the national enthusiasm over the incorporation of Austria into the German Reich was at its height, President Werner, the newly instituted plenipotentiary of Minister Kerrl, judged the moment ripe for putting into effect a demand which they had hesitated to place before the clergy till then, although it had been effected long since for officials and officers of the State and above all for the various organizations of the party: that is, their oath to the person of the Führer, Adolf Hitler. We must reflect that this National Socialist oath, according to the most explicit explanations, has a wider and completely different meaning from the oath which had once to be taken in Germany to the Kaiser and later to the Weimar Constitution, a much wider and completely different meaning from the oath to the standard, the vow, the obligation which was demanded and received from us in certain situations in the past. The oath to Hitler implies a total and unreserved, outward and inward obligation of the whole man (of his actions, his thoughts and his conscience) to this one man as the representative of the German State and the incarnation of the German people, and to his will, which is subject to no control or superior law. Werner's intention is that this oath shall be taken by all German clergy by May 31, 1938.

Let every man ask himself whether a Christian, and a preacher of the Gospel at that, can take this oath with a clear conscience? But then reflect, that it must be taken, under pain of deposition. And again, we might ask whether in these circumstances there would not be more than one Swiss Christian and clergyman who would take this oath. We who are not confronted by this test must at least understand the anxious questioning which is going through the ranks of the Confessing Church at this very moment: whether some middle way, avoiding this evil Either/Or, is not possible? On the basis of the Word of God? On the basis of this amazingly "totalitarian" State? By the time this *Kalender* appears, the decision will have been taken and will be known. It concerns one of the most serious crises that the Confessing Church has so far had to face.

A few attempts to come to the aid of the German Evangelical Church from outside are worth mentioning. In July 1937 the Ecumenical Church Conference met in Oxford and among other things sent a message to the Christians in Germany[1]. It was not exactly remarkable for decision and clarity, but it had a certain good effect in Germany on persecutors and persecuted alike. It was amazing and shaming, but also instructive, that the representatives of the German Free Churches

[1] See Duncan-Jones, pp. 309ff.

(Methodists and Baptists) at Oxford thought it right to take this opportunity of stabbing the Confessing Church in the back and assured the conference that the Gospel could be proclaimed in the Third Reich with complete freedom. The time will come when the still basically untouched German Free Churches (apart from the heavily persecuted sect of "Jehovah's Witnesses") will learn what this freedom really is. For the time being they have shown that, to be a true Church, it is not sufficient to be externally "free" from the State. Another freedom is really necessary, which the German Methodists and Baptists notoriously do not possess.

In this connection there may be mentioned the Swiss Relief for the Confessing Church in Germany, formed this year by a small circle, which has done modest yet useful work by the organizing of all kinds of hospitality for the tired and their dependants, and through a call for intercession during worship directed to the clergy and church authorities in Switzerland. Two books which are concerned with the German Church conflict, published in the summer of 1937 by Swiss authors: Dr. Arthur Frey and Pastor Rudolf Grob, have contributed, unfortunately in opposite ways, to further interest and participation in the events in Germany by more Swiss circles.

It is no accident that this time there is little to say of the inner life of the Confessing Church in Germany. No important synod or any other weighty public business in the Church has taken place. Responsible administration has been hindered not a little in its activity by various police measures and the illness of some of its members. The old inner contradictions within the Confessing Church are unfortunately still present and troublesome enough: between the established Church, whose organization was not destroyed in 1933 and which is thus not involved in the struggle and its promise, and those who are directly and actually suffering under the lie and use of force which broke out at this time. One could also say, between those who are concerned with the old Confession and those who are concerned with the confessing demanded today. Or, between those who like the Gospel for the sake of the Church and those who like the Church for the sake of the Gospel. It is most distressing that even Niemöller's case, instead of calling people to unity, did far more to bring this lack of unity to light. Who knows what else has got to be perpetrated by the opponent, so pitilessly single-minded in fact if not in method, in order to make peace in the Confessing Church itself, and therefore her power of decision and action, absolutely necessary.

But the real life of a Church is not contained only in what is visible in external Church politics (in a joyful or joyless manner). We often hear people among us ask whether the struggle and resistance of the Confessing Church in Germany will really keep going. We can depend on this: it is happening. It is happening on a very thin line, with much groaning and in much weakness. It must, because of its very nature, happen in the hiddenness of the life of each individual parish and in general in many single events and experiences, of which our papers say nothing and can in fact know nothing. But it is happening. By the grace of God it is true that the Church in Germany was allowed this year to feed privately and yet also quite openly on the bread which satisfies all hunger, to build on the ground which cannot subside, to be sheltered in the peace of God which passes all understanding.

The heavier attack that this year brought has shown all the more clearly (and despite the further encroachment on the nerves of all concerned which was mentioned in the last report) that between 1935 and 1937 something here and there has been learnt and grasped about the thing which will not be destroyed but will still shine brightly long after there has died away the great contempt and loud laughter at various other things which we can now regard as insurmountable. We shall also do good for our own sakes, praying and giving thanks that we are engaged in what is taking place in the Confessing Church in Germany, whatever form this may take.

THE GERMAN CONFESSING CHURCH 1938–39[1].

WHILE I ASK the readers of the *Zwingli-Kalender* for their attention again this year to what has happened among our evangelical brethren in Germany, I wish I could set before them a brighter picture than I can if I am to speak truthfully, as in the past years. But this time we can speak only with great anxiety. Anyone who does not like this may stop here. But a few are certainly prepared to share this anxiety.

The pressure under which the Confessing Church in Germany has to live has become noticeably heavier in the past year. Perhaps in relationship to the amazing momentum which German foreign policy has gained this year, there has been a certain haste to bring the very important incorporation (*i.e.* extermination) of the Church to its logical conclusion. But however that may be: this year everything has become much more threatening and testing than before. It is not a matter of bloody persecution of Christianity, as was once the case in Russia. That is certainly not the worst fate that can befall the Church. And the authoritarian state in Germany knows more effective means than that. It does not, or at any rate not yet, shoot the confessing Christians. The case of Martin Niemöller, held now in a concentration camp without sentence or justice for eighteen months, is an exception along with a few others of this kind (*e.g.* the case of the equally innocent Pastor Schneider of Dickenschied).

As a rule National Socialism uses quite different methods. To begin with, it threatened the life of the Church by trying to give its own meaning to the "unpleasant" doctrine. When this was only partially successful it aimed to silence this teaching by trying to destroy the Church's organization step by step. It deprives the Church of the possibility of ruling herself. It subjects her to a "neutral" executive machinery, which in reality serves its own totalitarian efforts exclusively. It gives the clergy and congregations superiors who have no conception of the Church and Gospel or who have conceived things solely as purged of Church and Gospel. It demands of them that they should

---

[1] *Zwingli-Kalender*, 1940. pp. 65–68. Written summer 1939.

treat Christian truth and the most evil pagan heresies as equally justified, not only in the pew, but in the pulpit too. It suppresses the Confessing authorities and the free theological colleges (as, finally, that of Bethel), which have become indispensable since the destruction of the theological faculties. It forbids examinations, ordinations, collections, publications, the whole press of the Confessing Church. It cuts off their post, their telephones, their meetings and announcements. It promotes (and on certain districts demands) that people leave the Church. Not only does it take the young people away from the Church, it even stirs them up against her.

One objection of good folk is: But those are all only externals. Of course they are only externals. But if the Church, like man, has not only a soul but also, according to the Bible, a body without which she can have no soul, *i.e.* without which her teaching cannot live and cannot sound forth, then it also means that, although this State cannot touch the Lord Jesus Christ, the Church which confesses to Him is on the point of being strangled. There can still be, as before, a hidden, completely inactive belief in the heart, but the Word of God can no longer be heard and powerful, it can no longer take on a living form.

And if the Church struggles against this death by strangulation, if she defends her body for the sake of her soul, maintains her organization for the sake of her teaching, then these same good folk say (even here in Switzerland!): "Niemöller 'preached politics' too much, and the Confessing Christians in Germany 'preach politics' too much, instead of proclaiming the pure Gospel!" As if that would be the pure Gospel which did not imply a visible bodily life of the Church, which could ultimately remain completely invisible in the world!

It is remarkable that what these good folk obviously want—a Church that is only inward and not at all outward—is identical with what National Socialism wants of the Church. For its attack is aimed directly at this very point, and this is where it raises its complaint. Every resistance against the death by strangulation intended for the Church is political rebellion. It fought this so-called rebellion with a whole machinery of suspensions, depositions, prohibitions of speech, imprisonments, confiscations, expulsions and such like, not counting the unofficial, but officially tolerated and desired, defamations of character, threats and molestations to which every single person who attempts to resist is subjected in the German publicity of even the smallest village. This sort of "persecution"—to which National Socialism in the opinion of these good folk obviously has every right—has made powerful strides in the past year and unfortunately achieved undeniable successes.

For it has become apparent that many in the ranks of the Confessing Church itself who four years ago would have been happy and ready to be shot for their faith were not equal to this sort of "persecution". I have already shown in previous reports that the question of confession in Germany today is largely a question of nerves. And it is just this bloodless but all the more energetic war on the Church that has got on the nerves of all who know their responsibility. The foreign policy with all its tensions, so extraordinarily sharpened this year, has also contributed to the creation of confusion. And so there came stagnation, defeats and retreats which were far more bitter than anything that the Gestapo could do to the Church. One of the best of the former leaders of the Confessing Church, a brilliant theological writer, rightly admired and loved by old and young alike, experienced some sort of conversion last year which had the practical effect of stabbing his former friends in the back.

Much curious talk was spread abroad of a "Christian suffering" which one must accept by becoming even more passive towards the attacking state than some members of the Confessing Church had unfortunately always been, and by breaking off one's struggle for justice and order in the Church and devoting oneself to parish work, still possible, even if in ruins. Moreover an inward aversion arose against something that the Confessing Church had till then maintained particularly strongly—the seriousness of theological work. This was to be replaced by a remarkable and neutral "simplicity," which in fact has the not at all simple but very clever power of calling black white, and white just as easily black. The sickness betrayed itself in the highly unhappy course of the affair referred to in the last report, the oath to be taken by the clergy to the Führer.

In retrospect, one can only say on this subject that in that unhappy weakening to which people fell victim, they were from the outset prepared to give way, *i.e.* to take the oath. Then they persuaded themselves very cleverly that this had been demanded of them by the State and that they had once again to be "subject to the powers that be". Finally, after the capitulation had been completed under this sign, they were ridiculed by the National Socialists, who said that no-one in the State and the party had thought of compelling the clergy to take this oath, not thanks to the fatal "Confession" synod of July 31, 1938, but in contradiction to it. Subsequently the affair has brought suffering to many. But so far no further synod has been found to make good that black day by an open admission of their mistake.

There was a further reverse in the autumn. The "Provisional Administration", the highest voice in the Confessing Church, had proposed during the Munich conference a service of prayer for the common day of prayer and repentance; a particularly important proposal in view of the threat of immediate danger of war. It contained among other things (what else could a day of repentance mean?) a confession of sin to be spoken in the name of the German people. This text was made known, aroused the displeasure of the party and led to police measures. The president of the Provisional Administration, Pastor Müller of Dahlem, has since lost his position and his livelihood because of this matter.

This was not the worst. What was bad was that on this pretext the quite well known bishops of the Established Church in Hanover, Bavaria and Württemberg once again left the north German Confessing Church in the lurch: a practical and human failure in loyalty that makes the necessary co-operation even more difficult than it always has been. But shortly afterwards a regrettable break occurred in Prussia itself. The National Socialist Church authorities there were attempting to gain control over the young clergy, examined and ordained by the Confessing Church, by offering to accept them into the official Church service and thus to give them employment and livelihood, on condition that they petitioned for it, let themselves be examined and admitted by them, and in future submitted entirely to their will. But out of 1,300 candidates only 150 accepted the offer. It was an older, and till then in his way equally venerable, leader of the Confessing Church who not only advised compliance in this matter but even brought about the yielding of a whole province and thus threw the whole front into confusion for a while. A Prussian synod held in January put an end to the danger so far as possible, with the agreement of the majority of the young men primarily concerned. But it seems that just after this synod many finally went back on themselves and joined the ranks of those who want to remain with half-hearted loyalty in the neutral "middle," where they think they can regard Church order as unessential.

Was the persecution of the Jews (and Jewish Christians) which broke out in November understood by the Confessing Church as the sign which it obviously was? In Thüringia (but, of course, in pious Württemberg too!) the result of these events was so far-reaching that the baptism of Jews is forbidden by the Church today. In practice more has been done for the persecuted Jews by individual Christians in the

74

parishes throughout Germany (but also by a special, efficient organization created for this purpose) than could be known in public and abroad. Admittedly many of the best people in the Confessing Church shut their eyes to the truth that the Jewish question, and thus the political question as such and as a whole, has become today a question of the faith. Luther's very dubious teaching on Matt. 28: 18, concerning the separation between the kingdom of Christ and all "wordly" spheres, lies like a cloud over the ecclesiastical thinking and action of more or less every course taken by the German Church. Will the Gospel in Germany (and elsewhere too) ever be really free from the Babylonian captivity of this teaching?

The opposition party of the "German-Christians," who had gradually sunk to a very unimportant factor in most districts, has surrendered to the leadership of its most radical wing, the Thüringian group, and now displays an extraordinary activity, even though it only represents a minority. Its preaching shows with greater clarity the partly sentimental, partly military, partly primeval, partly enlightening alien religion to which the Church in Germany (under the title of "German Faith"!) would have fallen prey, and would have to fall prey now, if the "Church struggle" had not been waged or were not carried on today.

The real danger and the worst enemy of the Confessing Church today is the army of neutrals in that non-confessing Church which is yet prepared for any compromise, *i.e.* the army of those whose symbol consists of two thick blinkers and whose ecclesiatical desire is to be dangerous to no-one, thus letting themselves be in no danger, who, to further this aim, are never at a loss for any possible patriotic, pious and learned argument and who above all have on their side the powers which in Germany today, as in all critical situations in world history, are humanly speaking the strongest precisely because they are so weak— illusion, fear and laziness. It is not impossible that there are many subjectively well-meaning persons in this army. But its watchwords (they all sound out a half-hearted loyalty) spell death. Pity the poor German Church and German people, if the Church struggle should ever end up in the lowlands of this "middle way".

And this is now the great question with which I must in all honesty close my report: Will the remnant of the former Confessing Church disappear one day into the ranks of this *"via media"* which has now gained an overwhelming majority? I can put this question only to deny it immediately with complete confidence. The Confessing Church is in the same position as were the troops of Gideon and often enough Israel also. She had to be sifted. The year 1938–39 was especially a period of sifting and perhaps this is not yet over. But we are continually hearing of moving proofs of loyalty and bravery, as they are quietly performed at many isolated outposts in the great struggle. And we hear that Martin Niemöller is holding out. . . . And if we were not to hear that? Then we would hear from the Word of God that He knows this people, that His congregations suffer and are oppressed and even deny themselves and Him and yet cannot completely die out. Then we have real reason and occasion to turn to Him who hears our prayers: Lord remember these thy congregations! and to know for sure that He will do so in one way or another.

INDEX

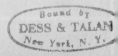